BLACK SAMSON

An African's Astounding Pilgrimage to Personhood

By Levi Keidel

Levi Keidel

Nov 26. 1975

Creation House
Carol Stream, Illinois

ISBN 0-88419-116-8

Library of Congress Catalog Card Number 75-22577

This book is dedicated to its central character
Maweja Apollo
whose conversion experience is no less remarkable
than that of the Apostle Paul . . .
whose cultural heritage, in richness and form,
parallels that of the ancient Hebrews,
and to
Ken Anderson
whose counsel on matters of
writing has been invaluable.

Publisher's Note

Like many other African countries, Zaire today is going through a period of strong national feeling. This is causing considerable concern among missionaries and mission organizations. Whether or not this new spirit of nationalism will hamper missionary activity is too early to say. But the time could come when believers like Maweja Apollo will be the only ones remaining to carry on the witness for Christ.

In light of this possibility the account appearing in the pages following becomes even more significant.

CONTENTS

I Throw Out a White Man

The year was 1943. I was a young man, about 23. I was working in a machine shop in a copper mine in the city of Kolwezi, in southeastern Zaire. The shop sat between two big sheds with furnaces to burn slag from the ore. It was a large house made of corrugated sheet iron; its high windows were dirty with slag dust. The air was heavy with the smell of burning minerals. Inside the shop, men stood or sat at their machines, doing their different kinds of work fixing things.

That morning I was seated at my table, working, as was my custom. I was washing burnt parts of an electric motor with gasoline. Then a white foreman arrived, and began doing what had become his daily custom.

"Has the baboon arrived?"

His words aggravated me exceedingly. On other mornings I had always answered him, as he desired. Today, I had sworn to myself that I would not. I sat quietly.

"Baboon?"

I refused to answer. I could feel his anger beginning to boil.

"What's the matter today? Are you trying to act like a white man? Look at your big lips and flat nose. Anybody can tell who you are. Answer me!"

I did not answer.

He slapped my face.

I stood and stared at him, my face stinging. My insides began

7

to boil with anger. This was not the first time I had been thus offended. On another day when I was high on the ladder, fixing a wire, a white man threw words at me from below which blackened my insides. I ran down the ladder. I threw my tools onto the table. I stood up to him, and burned him with my eyes. But I did not touch him.

This was the era when a black man dared not touch white men in anger; he touched them only to shake their hands. He didn't wear shoes on his feet, lest they accuse him of arrogance. He entered their houses to wash their clothes or to serve their drinks. Most of his speaking to them were the words, "Yes Sir." To break their laws was no light matter; black men were quickly imprisoned for upsetting the peace. Judgment was harsh. Its symbol was a whip made of a strip of hippopatamus hide, called a *mfeemboo*. From time to time offenders were flogged in public. In prison, some men wore iron collars padlocked around their necks. Dragging from them were chains nine feet long. Other men, when they entered prison, disappeared forever.

I knew all of these things. I was young; but my body was large and strong for its years. Must I accept forever for others to shame me because I was a black person? Does one judge a chicken by staring at its feet? Now my anger boiled up and overflowed my fears.

I seized this man's shoulders. I shook him like a leaf. What should I do with him? I wanted to fling him into the iron ceiling trusses above me. Instead, I laid him out on a table and held him down so he couldn't move. I glared at him until his eyes were like eggs, his beard trembled, and his face showed the fear of death. Then I picked him up, carried him to the door and, with all my strength, threw him out. He hit the ground, rolled over, stood himself onto his feet, and walked away.

After some minutes my director called me.

"What have you done?"

"I discarded a white man."

"When you threatened that other white man, I told you to restrain yourself. Do you want to lose your work?"

"I did not strike him."

8

"For what you have done, I am cutting one-half of today's wages."

"Good."

Because my mind fought over what I had done, the hours of the day passed quickly. One voice within me said, "You did well. You purged your insides, and now you feel clean." Another voice said, "Restrain your wrath. The lion by its anger rules its kingdom with terror; a tribal chief who thus governs people is held in contempt. If every time anger catches you, the lion within you breaks its restraining ropes, what might you be driven to do? How will you ever subdue it again?"

The workhorn sounded, startling me. It was time to go home. As I turned to leave my table, two black workmen came. One reached out to shake my hand.

"We pass each other day after day, but we haven't come to know each other. My name is Kabeya. Others saw what you did today. All of us respect you for your courage. We want to strengthen your heart. Why not come with us to a cafe where we can talk about our work affairs?"

"I am Maweja (*Ma-way-sha*)," I said, then greeted his friend. We walked in the direction of the workmen's camp and stopped at a hotel. Its front had a long veranda. Beneath it were small iron tables with wire-rod chairs. The house was divided into two parts: on the left, a large room for eating and dancing, and on the right a small room with a bar, stools and small tables for drinking. Behind the cafe was a row of small houses for sleeping. We joined five other young workmen at two tables put together on the veranda near the drinking room. Kabeya ordered beer for us. He told them who I was, and we shook hands.

"We saw a surprising affair today," he told the others. "Have you heard about it?"

"About the workman who beat up on the white man? We heard. Everybody is talking about it."

Others nearby stopped talking to listen.

"Our friend Maweja here is the one who did it."

"Truly?" Those at the table looked at me wide-eyed. Others brought their chairs and joined us. They looked at Kabeya.

9

"Tell us about it."

"Let Maweja tell us," Kabeya said.

All eyes fastened themselves to me. The table man was pouring our beer. Pride warmed my heart.

"I work at a table fixing electric machines. Every morning a white man passes my table. He always stops to offend me."

"You mean the little bearded one who always talks so fast?"

"We know him. His custom is to offend people."

"Go ahead."

"He has named me 'baboon.' He acts like he is taking roll call, and wants me to answer, 'Present.' The matter aggravated me exceedingly. This morning when I saw him coming, I told myself I would not answer. He stopped at my table and, as is his custom, said, 'Is the baboon here?'

"I kept doing my work quietly. I felt him glaring at me. Then he asked me again.

"I refused to answer.

"He put his hands on his hips to show his authority and cried out, 'Answer me!'

"I sat quietly.

"Then he started offending me. 'What's the matter today? Are you trying to imitate the white man? Look at your flat nose and big lips and see who you are. You stupid heathen.' Then he slapped me."

My listeners held their breath, waiting.

"Then I got up, seized his shoulders in my hands, and shook him. I could have killed him. But I decided to show him love. I laid him onto my table and held him there until his eyes showed me the fear of death. Then I carried him to the door, and threw him away like a dirty rag. He rolled over, got up, and left fast."

"Ayiiiiiiiiiiiiiiiiiiiii. . . . !" my listeners said. They leaped up, clapped their hands and cheered.

"Owner of courage!"

"You did excellently!"

"Maweja our hero!"

"What does his name mean? The all-powerful one!"

"Let's call him Mazungu . . . white man. Maweja Mazungu!"

"Raise your glasses! Let's drink to him as one man!"

10

I swallowed their praise with the licking of lips. Clearly, they longed as one with me, to throw off the yoke of humiliation put on us by the white man. They had chosen me as their path-cutter toward finding a way to do it. I accepted. My mind was so filled with their words of praise that it had no place for thinking where this path might lead me. All at once, without my planning it, I found I had chosen to follow this path, and others were already pushing me along it. The time arrived when it appeared I would pass through all the days of my life and still not finish paying for my choice.

Since this happened, many years have gone by. As I reflect upon it, perhaps my burden of shame did not begin with what was happening to us in the copper mine. Perhaps it began with matters of my tribal forefathers and of my childhood. Let me relate them to you, so that you will understand what made me choose this course, and how all the events before and after it fit together to make the picture of my life.

My Forefathers Were Cannibals 2

My father named me Maweja, "The all-powerful one"; it is part of a name our ancestors used to describe the Creator. Perhaps the heart of my father was sad because the ideas of people about our tribe prevented him from reaching the greatness he desired; so he hoped such greatness for his son. They had these ideas because of the way our tribe began.

Our forefathers were like vegetable leaves, picked from plants here and there, pounded in mortar, and cooked on fire until they are soft. The one who did these things to them was a black slave raider from a cannibal tribe which sat to the north of us. He came into our country to do his work during the days of my grandparents. His name was Ngongo Lutete.[1]

When Ngongo Lutete was a boy, Arabs from the far north raided his tribe and took him as their slave. He grew up serving them. He also became filled with their wisdom. It said that black people cannot be counted as human beings. They are worth less than four-footed animals. The only destiny suitable for them is death, mutilation or slavery that wears them down to the end of their breathing. As with livestock, to kill or to spare, either is good. When the Arabs saw that their teaching had made Ngongo Lutete bold and fierce, they gave him guns and put him to work catching people for them.

Ngongo Lutete was not heavy or tall. He had a small pointed beard; his lips were tight and narrow; his eyes red. He rode in a

12

large chair decorated with skins. It was tied between two heavy bamboo poles which were supported by carrying sticks on the shoulders of men, four in front and four behind. Ngongo dressed himself in clothes befitting his authority. He wore a long skirt with many folds; he decorated himself with small bells tied to his ankles, his wrists, and to the chair poles. His carrying-chair also was decorated with trophies from his victims.

From among his tribesmen Ngongo chose a group of seasoned warriors. They had exceedingly sharpened their skills of using weapons, but above all, of using the new fighting iron called "the gun." He made one of his tribesmen named Lupaka their chief.

Lupaka and his men always went ahead of Ngongo. If they found a village chief to be friendly, they asked him to give them warriors for their army. If they found him too strong to defeat in battle, they did as clever hunters who disguise themselves to catch their prey; they built huts by his village and lived there for months until, by cunningness, they won his friendship. If they found a chief who resisted them, they burned the village, caught people, brought an offering of people's heads to Ngongo, and ate meat from their corpses.

Few chiefs denied him what he wanted. His army grew. When he finally arrived at the place where he wanted to make battle, warriors from many tribes milled around him as thick as ants. They were itching constantly to fight. Their weapons were guns, bows, arrows, spears, large hacking-knives, and small stripping knives with carefully decorated handles and blades sharp as razors.

And so Ngongo Lutete, more cruel than a beast, made his war. His nose never ceased lusting for the smell of human blood. The people he caught from war to war, he tied with vines. Their number became so great that tieing vines became scarce. Other people he mutilated: he cut off lips, noses, ears, and tore out eyes to keep as trophies. Other people he made to stand in a row; he cut off their heads one at a time, while standing, making one pile of heads and another of bodies. Then the warriors would prepare baskets full of meat stripped from the bodies, to sell at the slave market. Most of all, Ngongo cherished tender meat; the meat of babies not yet born, taken from their dead mothers' stomachs.

They would take their captives and baskets of meat to a market gathering place to trade with other slave hunters for more guns. Ten persons were traded for a gun; one strong man was traded for two gun-loadings of powder; five women were traded for a handful of iron gun pellets; and one child was traded for a tin drinking cup, an empty bottle, or a large tin can.

What made them do such things? Greed. Greed for nothing; like that which makes a jackal pounce upon a field mouse.

He made war in this manner until the captured people were as many as his army could guard. Then he would march them far north to his capital city. Its high-walled fence was large enough to enclose living places for 15,000 people. Every fence post was covered with a person's skull. In his palace, he walked on a floor of bone, the tops of buried skulls. The corner-posts of his palace veranda were always splotched with fresh blood. Behind him, the earth was swept clean of living people, as a new broom sweeps chaff, not leaving a grain.

I do not say these things to horrify you. Other things I will not relate, lest you turn away from my words. I am describing for you a burden that my race has carried. Can I trust your understanding? On this earth all of us stand one height, like blades of grass. We all share the same end. The common white-haired village man whose wisdom is only that of the forest and field says, "The wisest witch doctor, in spite of all his magic medicines, will someday lie down with me, and we will die together."

My forefathers did not know how to write; they could not count the passing years. The army of Ngongo Lutete spread into our land about the year of 1890. Grandfather did not like to talk about it; he wanted to forget. I loved my grandfather. At times which I felt were fitting, I would ask him questions. Thus during the years of my childhood, he and my clan elders told the story by little pieces. These I put together.

It was early one morning, he told me. Creatures were already

14

stirring; it was already light. People were preparing to leave the village to tend their forest gardens. They had not yet learned about guns. The sky over their heads was clear. Suddenly something spoke, like a bolt of lightning. Terror caught them. They rushed out of the village climbing over the top of one another to escape. They fled toward the forest to hide, and threw themselves into the arms of Lupaka and his warriors. They were surrounded by the men of Ngongo Lutete.

The men of Ngongo did what their hearts desired that day. They butchered until they were weary, then they ate to the licking of bones. Grandfather was young and strong; he was spared. Those left living were bound. They were stripped of all clothing, to show that the whole of their bodies was healthy. A vine was wrapped around the neck of each person to make a tieing band. From these collars, vine cords about three steps long tied them together, two by two. Hands were tied behind their backs. Thus they passed the night.

When morning came they were made to stand, each two facing the same way. By means of the neck bands, poles were tied onto their shoulders. Upon these poles were tied food, gunpowder, iron pellets, and baskets of meat. Children still alive and old enough to walk, were tied by shorter vines to the waists of their mothers. Smaller children who bothered their mothers, were struck like a club against a tree, and discarded. They stood in the hot sun under their heavy loads until all were formed into a long line. Then they began their journey.

Ngongo Lutete continued making wars and catching people. After some days his slaves were great in number, from seven different clans. Then for one day, they rested. On the next day Ngongo and a large part of his warriors left. Those guarding the slaves said he went south to make the last war of this journey. After some days he would return, and they would all start following the footpath northward that led to his city.

The eyes of grandfather and his people saw these things; their bodies endured these things. How did all this make them feel inside? Grandfather never told me. But I know my people well; and from the years of my childhood, my heart and mind have drawn the picture for me.

I see several hundred of them sitting in the high grass beneath a grove of palm trees. It is late evening. The smoke of cooking fires still hangs low. They sit close together; they need the heat from each other to reduce the chill of night that is coming. They have already eaten, but their stomachs still gnaw with hunger. From carrying things, their bodies suffer knife-blades of pain. When they think about the tomorrows, their minds twist with fear. They cannot contain their suffering.

One weakly lifts his voice like a hurt animal, to chant his complaint. Another takes his turn. Then, as the unlocking of a hundred pent-up springs, they pour the bitter water of their hearts into one stream of agony, and lift their voices in a dirge song:

> Ngongo, who defies the Almighty,
> Who erases all feeling of shame;
> Who despises the love of a woman,
> The joy of fathering a child;
> Why did woman's womb bear you
> To pour horror and torment upon us?
>
> Wind that uproots every shade tree;
> Smoke that burns everyone's eyes;
> Curst be the night they conceived you.
>
> Fox who catches with cunning,
> Serpent who poisons the earth;
> Curst be the night they conceived you.
>
> Elephant crushing the helpless,
> Beast who makes all beasts to marvel;
> Curst be the night they conceived you.
>
> A beast eats all of its prey.
> You nibble, and leave corpses rotting.
> Curst be the night they conceived you.
>
> You pound lean meat in the mortar,
> Then stretch out each piece in the sunlight;
> Curst be the night they conceived you.

You set our home roofs on fire,
And roast people's limbs in their ashes.
Curst be the night they conceived you.

You cook dead men on your bonfires,
And living men under the sunlight.
Curst be the night they conceived you.

You eat our babies like goat meat,
Then sit back, picking your teeth.
Curst be the night they conceived you.

Your wickedness whitens our footpaths
With skulls, and ribs, and leg bones.
Curst be the night they conceived you.

We've used up all our words to describe you;
Our tongues are left dumb, and yet wanting.
Curst be the night they conceived you.

Tribemates whose spirits have left us;
Our tears flow down with your blood.
Rejoice in that place where you've gone;
Where the sun will not rise on tomorrow.

Tshiyamba is Sacrificed 3

A guard named Katombe watched the captives. They passed each day in great fear, as snared animals awaiting the arrival of the snare owner. The day for Ngongo's return came and passed. When there was no more food, Katombe sent guards with slaves to get cassava from fields near villages they had destroyed. He had others make palm-frond shelters to protect people from rain. He loosed the bonds of a few women each day to prepare palm oil and to gather greens for cooking. Bit by bit, the fear of Ngongo's return was washed from their minds, as the tears of a weeping woman slowly wash the face.

A month passed. It became clear to everyone that they could not continue this way forever. The day was coming when Katombe would have to make a decision. Clan leaders among the slaves whispered with one another when they were not being guarded closely; they formed a plan, and waited.

One evening, the sun already having set, slaves were given larger portions of food. They ate. Guards began to make them lie down to sleep early. Slaves with more courage kept asking them why. Finally a guard said, "You will need strength. When day breaks, we begin our journey."

"Where are we going?" Those who heard the guard's words fastened their eyes upon him.

"We are going to meet those waiting for us."

The word spread like fire driven by wind through dry grass. Clan leaders knew that on such a journey, many would die. Others would become ill and, after arriving, would also die. At this point they had one word in their hearts: "The forefathers said, 'What is the difference whether the witch doctor kills you with flea bites, or with poverty? The chicken who sees the knife and pot knows what is going to happen.' Now is the time to have courage and speak. If we die, we die."

"Let us speak with Katombe," one said.

"Yes. Take us to Katombe!" answered other clan leaders. The words caught the lips of everyone: "We want Katombe! Let Katombe come." Guards began striking a few people, but the captives would not be silenced. Katombe, in his hut, knew by listening that this was no meaningless uproar. He heard his name. Through darkness that now made everyone look the same, he came, and stood at the edge of the circle of people.

"What do you want?" he shouted.

Even the insects became silent. Then a clan leader brave enough to die spoke in the darkness.

"Is it true that we begin the journey tomorrow?"

"Yes."

There was more silence of waiting.

"Do you know this journey will be a success?"

"Why would it not be?"

Sufficient silence appealed for Katombe's respect.

"Have you gathered enough food for this many people for such a long journey?" one asked.

Another followed. "If we raid the fields of others along the way, will they not attack us? You and your helpers have only a few guns and hand weapons; will that be sufficient to defend us?"

"Some of us will die on this journey," said another. "With the passing of sufficient days, others of us will truly arrive. But if when we arrive, we find that Ngongo was slain in war, what will we do? The journey will have been for nothing."

Katombe was silent. Slaves hoped this meant he was perplexed. Finally he spoke.

"What are you asking for?"

"We know that you are troubled," said the first one. "You are as a wren sitting alone on a grass stem after a prairie fire. You want your chief. But we have watched you. You know how to take care of people. You may take us tomorrow. Suppose after many days, you lose many of us and find your chief. Then will your heart truly be happy? The elders say, 'Feed animal entrails to a lion long enough, and it will return to consume you.' Do you think you will serve Ngongo happily forever?"

Quietness.

"What do you want to say?" Katombe asked.

"Which is better? For you to be the servant of Ngongo who may someday betray you; or to be chief of people who want you?"

People stopped breathing and waited. Katombe was thinking hard.

"If I were your chief, what would you pledge me?"

Words of clan leaders ran one over the top of another.

"We would pledge ourselves to be your people forever."

"We would not desert you. Where would we go?"

"We would pour the oil of anointing upon you, and upon your sons who follow you."

"We would sit here as one people, and build the kingdom of Katombe."

Katombe paused. Within him these words were writing themselves clearly. Then he took his guards to one side and began talking with them. People waited, fear battling their hope. Finally, through the darkness spoke the voice of Katombe.

"Greetings. If your pledges are true, so be it."

No one could sleep that night. When day came, Katombe sent guards with a gun to hunt a male sheep and other food animals. They returned when the sun was past half its journey. The seven clan leaders shed the sheep's blood and, with it, sealed the covenant of Katombe's chieftainship. From one of its horns, they poured the oil of anointing upon his head. Then they carried him on their shoulders to a tree. He mounted himself onto its big limbs and with a loud voice, declared the authority of his chieftainship. Clan leaders cried out in assent, and bowed to the ground before him. Then guards cut off the bonds which remained. That evening, women prepared a feast. Everybody partook of the covenant food. Then they danced in celebration of their joy, not watching the time, into the darkness, until their strength was finished.

X   X   X   X

Our people abandoned their palm-frond shelters. They built huts of mud walls and grass roofs. They planted their fields; they bore their children. Katombe was a strong chief, ruling his people well. As one plants a peanut in the ground and, later, pulls up a handful, so our people multiplied.

The passing of years washes away the colors of memory. The way my people had suffered under Ngongo Lutete began to fade; their promise to sit as one person under Katombe began to fade. Clan leaders began competing for power, each wanting to make himself a chief. Then came fighting. Bloodshed, beginning as a rivulet, grew into a stream that wanted to wash them all away. One day Katombe called the clan leaders, sat them down before him, and spoke.

"Many rain seasons ago, when you wanted to make me chief, I had hard thoughts," he began. "No one had ever heard of a stranger becoming chief of slave captives from mixed tribes. Also, our hands were empty. But your pleading softened my heart, and I accepted. Then by working hard, we did an amazing thing. As maggots, without a knife, butcher an elephant carcass, so we, with nothing, built our tribe.

"But now it appears you have forgotten that I had pity on you. You have forgotten that it was your hands which poured upon my head the anointing oil; it was your mouths which spoke the words that you would sit in peace and together build the kingdom of Katombe. These many years, as one family, we have slept under the same roof. If you have not forgotten your promises, why do you now speak words which split the house?"

Clan leaders sat looking at the ground in shame, as dogs caught stealing meat.

"Under the chieftainship of Ngongo, some of you would

21

have lived. Shall people say that under the chieftainship of Katombe, everyone died? Will you wipe yourselves from the earth, and at the same time, bring such shame upon me? No. I will not accept it. Each of you must look hard into the customs of your forefathers. Together, we must carry out a strong covenant. The blood of those you have killed is crying from the earth. Our covenant must be strong enough to silence it. The covenant we make must bring an end to bloodletting, and show all generations following us that we are a tribe of peace."

When shame subsided, clan leaders began looking at one another. They agreed on what they must do. Then their hands worked, while their hearts, as dumb sentinels, watched.

One day a covenant feast was prepared. They chose a large open space between the path where bypassers walked, and the first row of houses. They cleaned and swept it. In the center of it they dug a large deep hole, heaping the fresh brown dirt around its edge. The people of each clan brought a live goat; a throwing spear; an innocent virgin girl; and cassava flour to prepare mush for the feast. Before eating together, they would seal their covenant. Every person of Chief Katombe was to be present, or bear the penalty of death.

Chief Katombe sat on his chieftainship chair, the hole remaining to his right. His leopardskin of authority was across his knees. A strong servant stood on each side of him. Seven clan leaders sat on low stools in a circle before him; each had a spear and a bound goat at his feet. Seven young girls stood quietly in a line along the other side of the hole, facing the chief. In the open space encircling them all, packed as tightly as dried grass stems on a hut roof, stood the people of Katombe.

The chief drew lots to choose one of the girls. The lot caught a girl named Tshiyamba. Katombe made her stand before him.

"Our child Tshiyamba, this is your day of glory. As of today, all of us you see standing here wipe from our memories forever the names of our clans. It is your honor to be founder of a new tribe of people, the tribe of Tshiyamba. We who look upon you with our eyes, bind ourselves in a covenant never to be broken, to honor you forever, and to live as one tribe in peace. Because of what we do today, our children and our children's children will call themselves by your name, and will sit in peace and happiness. Heaven and earth, witness our oaths."

Katombe nodded to his servants. They covered the girl's eyes with a cloth, and tied it. They laid her on the ground. One tied her hands, quietly speaking words of comfort to her. The other tied her feet, his hands wanting to tremble. The hearts of all watching them trembled. The servants lifted Tshiyamba, sat her down into the center of the deep hole, and returned to their places. The chief cried with a voice loud enough to enter every ear:

"Earth under our feet; upon you all living beings walk; from you all living things eat. We have done you badly. We have drained upon you the blood of our tribemates. They died for nothing. Their blood cries for vengeance. Today, may its cries be appeased and silenced forever. We now drain upon you this innocent blood to cover our guilt. Accept this sacrifice which we offer you, and let peace again come between us."

Then he cried to his people, "May this shed blood appease the earth for our fighting!"

"So be it!" cried the people.

"May it cleanse us of our evil!"

"So be it!"

"May it bind us together as one thing!"

"So be it!"

"May it seal our oaths forever!"

"So be it!"

Then the clan leader on the chief's right rose, took his goat to the hole, slashed its throat, and drained its blood into the fresh ground. Each other leader followed in his turn.

A piece of meat was cut from each carcass and cooked in one pot. A portion of cassava flour from each clan was cooked in another. When the food was prepared, clan leaders sat closely in a little circle around the two pots, and Katombe said:

"May the one who eats with enmity in his heart toward another be cursed and die."

"So be it!"

"Make your vows to the earth; show it that there is no longer anger among us."

Each clan leader in his turn, broke a handful of cassava mush off the loaf in the pot, and threw it into the hole. Then they sat down together and ate the food.

Again the chief cried out, his hands gripping the chair arms tightly.

"Is fighting among us finished forever?"

"It is finished!"

"Before the Great Elder Spirit, pronounce your oaths to the earth."

Each clan leader, one after the other, took his weapon of war, broke its staff, and laid it in the hole beside Tshiyamba.

Then Katombe turned his chair to face the hole. Clan leaders knelt around the edge of the hole, and lifted loose dirt in their hands. A woman began to mourn. Katombe stood slowly and spoke, his voice like that of an animal in pain.

"Tshiyamba, our vows have entered your ears. Your ears are the ears of the earth. Your spirit will live in the earth forever. We have made our peace now. Should any one among us raise his hand to break our peace, may the earth swallow him in vengeance. May your spirit destroy him. May his seed be cursed to perpetuity."

"Shall it be thus?" he asked his people.

"Let it be thus!"

Each clan leader threw his handful of dirt onto Tshiyamba.

The servants closed the hole, with everybody watching.

Thus one gave her life to finish our evil and to reconcile us again. Since that day, our people, under Chief Katombe and his descendants, have called themselves "The Tribe of Tshiyamba," and have lived in peace.

I Learn about "The Great Chief"

While a small child at home, I was as content as a peanut hooked to its stem. When one first appears upon earth, he becomes familiar with his parents, his relatives, and the customs they already have established for him to follow. These things are woven around him in such a way that he entrusts himself to them, and so finds contentment. These things might be compared to a carefully woven bag, made to carry things for a long journey. It carries good and bad things equally well. I must now help you to understand the fabric of the bag which was to carry me on my earthly journey.

Before the coming of the white man, each large village or group of small villages was a kingdom by itself. Because of fighting between kingdoms, we could not travel far. We could not trade with distant villages. We lived using only the things we found near us. We were poor. We fought constantly against enemies which wanted to destroy us: hunger, sickness, sometimes warriors from neighboring tribes. All the cleverness of our minds and all the strength of our bodies were made to work for us, that we might stay alive. For this reason, our forefathers developed customs which would strengthen our tribe and tie us together as one thing. This explains why it was necessary for Tshiyamba to die.

Strength is in large numbers. We needed many in our tribe to make fields for food, and to go to war; thus we would overcome our enemies. And so the elders say, "Man loves a woman to bear children." Every adult person was expected to help replenish our tribe and multiply its numbers.

Thus a man with more than one wife was a man of honor; by this means he bore into the tribe a large number of children. Our chief had many wives, so that his blood would be more widely dispersed among us. Rarely did a young man marry a woman of another tribe; we married one another.

Marriage covenants were sealed with the paying of bride price. A proverb says that a woman married without bride price is like a hen; she'll desert her young and go elsewhere as soon as they start pecking for themselves. This custom of paying bride price kept a man and his wife bound together. With the passing of time, the blood which flowed in the veins of our chief whom we all honored, and the blood of every newborn baby, was one. The commonness of our blood became the mortar which bound us together like a wall, strong, straight and firm.

Our forefathers also agreed on rules for dealing with affairs which would weaken our tribe. A liar was one who betrayed his tribe and brought shame upon his clan. A proverb says, "The penalty for one who steals is hard; if he's your child and flees, we will punish you." If a child stole again and again, the father would burn off the ends of his fingers to mark him forever. If the clan could not correct his stealing, it would renounce his family, or the chief would sell him as a slave to another tribe.

Our forefathers believed that men and women lying together promiscuously would ruin the tribe. They had strong laws which made sexual union sacred. Many times those committing adultery were killed. A young man who ruined a girl's virginity was required to pay her parents a bride price and a fine, and to take her as wife. Children who did such things to each other in play, or who viewed their parents' nakedness, were judged by the full tribal council; a white chicken was killed, and its blood was sprinkled on their legs to cleanse them. If they refused to confess such sin, their powers to reproduce were bound. If a parent lay with his child, at night both were taken and thrown into the river to die.

To restrain the body's desire to do such evil, girls approaching womanhood could not sleep together. Parents could not bathe or sleep with their older children. Thus the gift of each man and each woman was kept strong and pure. Because such things were taboo between a child and his parents, we spent much time with our grandparents. We learned from them important things about life.

As a wall finds its strength in tightly-packed bricks, so the tribe found its strength in closely-bound families. People of a family were tied together as snugly as a bundle of straight sticks. They always felt the needs and strengths of one another. When one was disturbed, others knew it.

Thus if I needed something, my father and his brothers would combine their wisdom and strength to get it for me. Stinginess found no place in their thinking. If I became ill, these men, all of whom I call my fathers, would do whatever was needed for me to recover. When I lacked money to go on an important journey, they would provide it. When it was time for me to marry, each of them would contribute animals, cloth, or other needed wealth to make up the bride price. If I were disabled, they would feed and clothe me. My father carried an equal burden to see that the needs of his brothers' children were met.

No affair happened which could be hidden in a corner; no one was left alone with his problems; everyone worked with him to solve it. If a man's wife was barren, relatives assembled wealth to pay a medicine man to follow customs necessary to unlock her powers of birth. If such customs failed, the man's fathers helped him pay bride price for another wife with powers to bear. If a man died, his eldest brother took the widow to meet her needs and to bear children by her.

When a child was rebellious, or when a woman argued with her husband, the oldest living man member of that family carried the burden to resolve the problem. This was generally the grandfather. If the problem was too hard for him, it was discussed by a council made up of the eldest member of each family of the clan. If they could not resolve it, the tribal council, made up of clan leaders and the chief, would judge it.

Thus, as the baby draws all its strength from its mother's breast, so each child among us grew up drawing all his needs from the sticks which lay next to him in the family bundle. When he matured, he became in turn a source toward providing the needs of his children and brothers. Thus during my growing-up years, my family was my succor; my tribe was my defense. To be disloyal to them was to destroy oneself. The fortune of one of us was the fortune of us all; and none among us would ever die because he was poor or alone.

My grandfather was very important to me. He wove together for me many pieces which were to make up the journey bag of my life.

"Where did our ancestors come from?" I asked him one time.

"I pass on to you the story told me when I was a child," he said. "Long long ago when the hills were still new, our ancestors lived in the far north country. They were all one people. They all spoke the same tongue. They were planting their gardens and eating the forest animals. They believed they had subdued the earth; so they started questioning one another about reaching heaven.

"They tied long sticks together and packed them with mud so as to make a tall tower. When it finally reached high into the sky, people crowded onto it. So many people climbed up it that it broke, and fell to the ground. The hearts of all of them split with fear. They got up and fled; three ran this way, four ran that way. They discovered themselves talking languages they could not understand. Black people came this way southward. Others of them, becoming weary, stopped here and there along the way. We, being stronger than others, came to the far south and stopped in the land where we are today."

Another time I was hoeing with him in the field. Part of the story of Ngongo Lutete's evil acts made me think hard that day. When we entered the path to return home, I asked, "Evil that enters into man's heart to make him like Ngongo Lutete, where does it come from?"

"Our ancestors told us that long ago the eldest and greatest of all living spirits made a field," he began. "He wanted his creatures to be happy. So he gathered all the insects which bite us and make us ill, and locked them inside the fruit of a tree. Then he created the first man and woman. He told them to till the field and to eat of its plants; but they were not to eat the fruit of that one tree.

"One day while the man was away working in the field, the woman became very thirsty. She picked the fruit and opened it to drink the juice. All the insects rushed out of it; they stung her on the body and made her very ill.

"When the man returned to the hut that evening, he discovered what the woman had done. He was so angry he deserted her. He wandered the earth looking for a helper who would be obedient. He found no one to cook for him. He had not one to talk to. He returned. The woman lured him to taste the fruit. He ate it, and sickness caught him as well. That evening the Chief of the field came looking for them. He found them hiding behind their hut, lying with their faces to the ground in shame.

"The Great Chief followed the palaver. He wanted to find out which of his creatures was guilty of tricking the woman into eating the fruit. He found it was the snake. He was so angry with the snake he cursed it; He cut off its arms and legs, and discarded it in the high grass. From that time, the snake has been crawling on its belly, abhorred of men, as you see it today."

I listened carefully. I was as an innocent child sitting on a river bank taking mind-pictures of the passing stream.

A Diviner Determines Adultery 5

It is not important that I tell you all the affairs of my childhood. My forefathers would eat the pieces of cassava mush they needed, and throw the rest into the high grass for the spirits to eat. And so, I will share with you only the pieces of my childhood which later revealed themselves to be important, and will discard the rest. I will build my words around two affairs: the troubles of an uncle, and the kindheartedness of my father.

The man and woman who live together for many days know that their hut roof covers many things. Generally one roof is sufficient. But the affair between my father's youngest brother Beya and his wife Ndaya became too strong for their hut roof to cover. When sufficient days passed, their problem troubled the whole village, and ended at the feet of my father.

Beya and Ndaya were married for three years. They had no children. To any man among us, this is shame. The heritage which remains on earth after him is his offspring. As the fathers say, "A bird rises into the sky and leaves its cry; a man goes into the ground and leaves his child." The family fathers were following tribal customs one after another to resolve the problem. Then one evening, arguing split the house roof. People saw Beya leave, his fists clenched, his face black as night. He went across the village to the home of a friend he had grown up with whose name was Kanda. There was a fight. Kanda's cheek was cut.

The following morning, when the sun began to warm the earth, Leta, our old and respected chief, the son of Katombe, called a meeting of the tribal council. Their meeting place was beneath a large tree at one end of the long open space between the footpath of bypassers, and the first row of village houses. Chief Leta took his place on a chair by the tree. His two servants stood behind the chair, their arms folded, their bare chests showing their strength. Members of the tribal council were clan leaders. Elders from the families of Beya, Ndaya and Kanda, also were present. Sitting on low stools, they stretched in a straight line on each side of the chief, as a taut bow-string leaves each side of the finger pulling it. Across the ends, like a bow, gathered the people, all of them, some sitting, some standing, as milling bees drawn by honey. My uncle Beya, his wife Ndaya, and Kanda were guarded at a distance where they could not hear.

Chief Leta spoke to a servant. He left, and brought Beya. The people became quiet. The chief spoke:

"Beya, we hear that you and Kanda fought last night. What was the affair?"

"He is committing adultery with my wife."

The words hit people's hearts like a heavy stone.

"Such an accusation is no light matter. You know the penalty for such evil."

"I know it."

"What evidence do you have to show that Kanda is guilty?"

"In past weeks my wife has been sending to his hut gifts of freshly-cooked cassava mush. Three days ago when I came from my field at evening, I caught him leaving my hut. Last evening I found he had brought her the gift of a freshly-killed partridge."

Village women looked at one another, their mouths open in amazement.

"Have you seen any other sign which shows you that your wife desires other men?"

"Yes. Those days of each month when she is unclean after the

31

custom of women, she stays in the high-grass hut prepared for such women, as is the tradition of our ancestors. But for two months, when the days of her uncleanness are past, she has come to live in my house again without offering me cooked white meat to show that she is pure."

"Have you seen anything else?"

There was silence. Then slowly the face of Beya darkened, his anger wanting to boil.

"Once we were arguing because she has born me no children. She offended me. She said it was my fault that she could not bear. I was not as other men. I did not have strength to make her conceive."

People burned their eyes on Beya. Fingers tapped cheeks in wonder.

"Has there been any other sign?"

"No."

Father's brother Beya was made to stand to one side. The servant brought Kanda. Black medicine had dried his cheek wound.

"Why did fighting appear at your house last night?"

"Beya accused me of ruining his wife."

"Do you have friendship with Ndaya his wife?"

"Only the friendship of persons."

"You have never known her in any other way?"

"I have never had it in my heart to do such a thing."

"You are lying!" Beya jabbed toward him with a finger. "Before I married her you said that if you had sufficient bride price you would steal her from me!"

"Hush! You finished your words," clan leaders together rebuked him.

Leta raised his hand to quiet the people, then spoke.

"Is it true that Ndaya has been sending cooked food to your house?"

"Yes."

"For what reason?"

"Sickness has been plaguing my wife these past weeks. Sometimes she cannot cook. She and Ndaya have been friends since childhood. Ndaya is not happy for us to sit in hunger. She sends us food."

"Were you in the hut of Ndaya the evening of three days ago?"

Kanda looked far away, remembering. "On that day my wife was ill in bed. She asked that I return Ndaya's cooking pot. I did not enter the hut. I gave it to her at the door."

"Have you sent Ndaya a gift of meat?"

"No."

"Do you know anything about a freshly-killed partridge?"

"Yes. Yesterday morning Ndaya sent us word that she would cook the evening meal for us. I was in the high grass during the afternoon, and found that one of my snares had caught a partridge. I brought it to Ndaya to cook for us for supper."

There was a pause.

"Now what about the words of Beya? Did you tell him you would steal his bride?"

"Perhaps I did. But how do boys talk with one another when they see a pretty girl?"

When it was agreed that there were no more questions, Kanda was made to stand to one side opposite Beya. The servant brought my aunt, Ndaya.

"Are you the friend of Kanda?" the chief asked.

"We have been friends since our childhood."

"Do you have friendship with him of any other kind?"

"No."

"Is it true that you have been sending cooked food to his house?"

"Yes. Why should I not? His wife is my good friend. She has been ill. Should I leave them sit in hunger?"

"Has Kanda ever come to see you when your husband was not at home?"

"He came three days ago; but that was to return my cooking pot."

"Has Kanda brought you meat?"

"Yes. Last evening he brought me a partridge to cook for them."

There was a pause for thinking.

"Ndaya, if you have been cooking for your friends these many times, how is it that you have not told your husband?"

She licked her lips preparing her words.

"He doesn't know how his scoldings eat out the heart of his wife; to him his words are like birds having taken flight."

"Have you ever said anything to your husband that would show him you desire the love of another man?"

"Why would I say something like that? I have even put tshipambu medicine on his food to turn his heart around to desire me. Why would I refuse him?"

"Have you ever accused Beya of not having the strength of men?"

Her face blackened and appeared to harden as stone. "I said those words in anger."

"Is it true that you no longer give him white meat from month to month to show him you are pure?"

Ndaya looked hard at her feet. Her bottom lip protruded with defiance. She said nothing. The judges pondered her words. Chief Leta fixed his eyes upon her as arrows pointed to the heart, and spoke.

"It is the burden of us who are over you to fix up our village troubles so that we may sit in peace. As the elders say, a traveller does not lie to those showing him the way. When the time is sufficient, all evil reveals itself. Speak truth. Though you hide yourself under water to eat stolen peanuts, the floating hulls will betray you. You must tell us your heart."

Ndaya turned her eyes to the ground again and said no more.

The servants took the three away. The tribunal judges and family elders pondered and debated for a long time the words they had heard. Finally it was agreed what must be done. Beya, Kanda and Ndaya were brought. Ndaya was called to stand before the judges. The chief spoke.

"Ndaya, in this palaver there are two affairs which we must deal with: the accusation of adultery, and the shedding of blood in anger. Our tribal elders had one word about unfaithfulness under a hut roof; a woman of light morals is worth no more than ten grasshoppers and a cricket leg. In this matter the burden is ours to establish the truth.

"You say you are innocent. The words of you and Kanda fit as a thread prepared to fit a needle eye. Some among us think that you and Kanda may have prepared these words together beforehand to cover up your evil. Some of your acts in the home do not show that you are innocent. Putting the words of all of you together, we are not able to establish the truth. There is a proverb which says, 'If you want to prove that you have no lice in your hair, shave your head.' If you are innocent, we want to clear your name of this evil. Are you willing to undergo the iron-bracelet truth test?"

Fear struck her face. She looked hard at the ground and pondered. Then slowly her face began to show strength. Finally she said quietly, "Yes."

Our tribal diviner and a helper prepared things quickly. They brought two cooking pots. The smaller one contained medicine made of pounded leaves of a forest plant mixed with cool water. It was placed to one side. The larger pot was partly filled with water. It was placed on a fire. When the water began to boil, enough cassava and corn flour were stirred into it to make a thin mush, almost filling the pot. The diviner was seated. Ndaya was made to stand before him. He placed the boiling pot before him, and spoke.

"Ndaya, the accusation of adultery has split your hut. Your husband says you are guilty. You say you are innocent. What we are about to do will establish the truth."

He unfolded a cloth on the ground beside him, and drew out a bracelet made of black twisted iron.

"What we do now does not begin with us; it began with our forefathers. You will bathe your hand in the pot of divining medicine. I will drop the bracelet into the boiling mush. You will put your hand into the mush, hunt the bracelet, draw it out and drop it into the medicine pot. If you are guilty, the flesh of your hand will come out scalded. If you are innocent, the flesh of your hand will be unharmed. Do you have anything to tell us before I drop the bracelet?"

"No," Ndaya said, staring at the large pot.

The helper made Ndaya kneel before the pots. He put her right hand into the cool-water pot, rubbing onto it the divining medicine. Then she turned toward the boiling pot, waiting. Every eye was fastened to it. The diviner held the bracelet over the pot, looked at Ndaya one more time, then dropped it.

"Reach for it!"

Ndaya's face hardened. She thrust in her hand, searched a moment, pulled out the bracelet, and thrust her hand into the cool medicine pot. The helper washed off her forearm and held it into the air for all to see. It was unharmed. Village women cheered.

After people were quieted, my uncle Beya was called. He looked only at his feet.

"Ndaya has established for us her innocence," the chief said. "It remains for us to deal with the matter of shedding blood in anger. When this affair began to blacken your insides, why did you not bring it to the elders of your clan whose work it is to judge such things? Does this not show disrespect for those over you? The forefathers said, 'Better let anger burn your Adam's apple than spill it upon a brother! You spilled your anger upon a tribal brother, and wounded him. In this matter, you are guilty.

"You know the penalty handed down to us for such an act: death for death, burn for burn, wound for wound. The ancestral spirits will not restore peace to our village until their law is executed. By this means we will also strengthen our respect one for another."

Leta gestured with his grey beard. His servants bound Beya's hands before him, and laid him on the ground. One servant held him. Kanda was made to sit on a stool beside him. The other servant, with a narrow strip of bamboo, carefully measured the length of Kanda's cheek wound. He laid the bamboo strip on the same place on Beya's cheek. Then with a small stripping knife, he cut the same wound onto the cheek of Beya. Then Beya was released.

Thus the work of the tribunal was finished. It remained to give counsel to those who were wrong. Beya and Ndaya were of one clan. One of their clan leaders spoke.

"Beya, your marriage is not the matter of you alone. You chose this woman, and we gathered her bride price. Your marriage is the concern of all of us. The elders say, 'Choose your wife carefully and stick to her; she's not a piece of cheap cloth you can change at will.' You will pay her a large rooster for the way you have troubled her. The bow and arrow separately can do nothing. They work together. Each respects the work of the other, and thus they feed the tribe. So take your wife Ndaya. Work together with her; and thus build the honor of our tribe.

"Ndaya, marriage is a basket man must use to cross the stream. A careless woman upsets it. Be a woman of wisdom. Curb your tongue from fanning fires. You have chased from our minds the thought that you were unfaithful; do nothing that will make us recall the thought. Return to your hut. Your husband is not an uncircumcised alien. Respect him. Do faithfully the duties of a wife, and sit in peace."

The people looked at one another and nodded their heads.

"Justice has been done today," they said.

Each person went to his hut.

My Father's Many Wives 6

The troubles of my Uncle Beya progressed until they arrived at the doorstep of our house. But before I tell you how they ended, I must describe for you the heart of my father.

Our ancestors related to us stories of the past which help explain the kind of wisdom which ruled their hearts. For example, they told us that one day long ago, the sun rose as is its custom. Then, in the middle of daytime, it became dark as moonless night. Chickens didn't understand the time, and went to roost. Then all at once, the earth shook like a leaf in the wind. Men's hearts split with fear. They asked one another what had caused it.

After a long time, they learned that this was the day people killed the Child of the Great Elder Spirit. Of all peoples of earth, only this child created Himself. The name our forefathers gave Him shows that He had weapons and the power to wage war; but He refused to use them, and died. Because they killed Him, His Father, the Great Elder Spirit, was angry; He covered the face of the sun and shook the earth.[3] He gave His Child life again, so that the Spirit of His Child is still wandering on the earth. And so up to today, there is a proverb which says, "Don't be stingy with the orphan; feed and clothe him; he is the child of the Eldest Spirit."

It is for reasons like this that our forefathers cared for

orphans and widows, fed the hungry, and clothed the naked. The offering of Tshiyamba brought an end to our fighting and made us people of peace. After that, if a person left another tribe and came wanting to sit among us, our people welcomed him. They gave him a place to build his hut; if he was single, they helped him find a wife from among us; they gave him a place to make his fields; they called him "sir." They were generous, courteous and polite.

Father followed their footsteps. He was known among our people for the love and happiness he showed to everybody. Through all the years of my childhood he taught me incessantly, "Take good care of your body. Guard your reputation. Always be kind to the person sitting with you. When he asks for something, don't turn your back; giving is storing; someday it will return to you. Give it to him. Respect him. Love him. Obey him. Don't touch his wife. Don't steal. Welcome guests. If you think strangers may be in the village, at mealtime leave a bowl of food along the path outside the hut; better feed a full stomach than deny a hungry man something to eat. Try to do good to everybody."

Father taught us to work. When the eating of termites weakened a wall post, he replaced it. When a grass roof began to leak, he repaired it. He gave us children the work of sweeping our yard and putting things in order each morning. When the boy children of our family became older, he helped us build a living-hut for ourselves. He gave me a baby goat and told me to take good care of it and raise it as my own.

He taught us our lessons of hardest work in his fields. "If you respect your stomachs, you'll respect work in the fields; they feed us," he would say. During the years of my childhood, father took to himself four wives. Through the months of every year they did the kinds of work that all women perform for their husbands: splitting wood, fetching water, gathering greens, cooking food, making wine, preparing palm oil. But each year when the rainy season approached, he sent us all to the prairies. He saw that our hoes ate the high grass. We planted; we weeded; we harvested. There was never hunger at our house. We had manioc, corn, beans, peanuts and sweet potatoes; our cooking pots were always full. Father helped all his brothers marry; their bride prices came from things sold from our fields. Other produce was traded at the marketplace, and brought us the things we needed.

Through the years, father became recognized for his good deeds and hard work. His wives, and the wealth they helped him gather, made him highly honored. Tribal leaders promoted him. They chose him to be chief of a clan of nine families. They chose him to be responsible to arrange affairs for guests coming to the village for important events such as mournings, tribunals and consultations between tribal chiefs. Thus when persons arrived, he would distribute among them the things they needed: food and sleeping places. Father was given a long name which meant, "If you can detour hunger, all that's left to detour is death."[4]

Thus you can understand why the journey bag of my childhood carried me contentedly; a large piece of it was woven by my father. But even though two knife blades are sharpened on the same honing stone, they don't cut the same. If Father's life caused people joy, the life of his brother Beya continued to cause everyone sorrow.

Because the tribunal had found him guilty, he carried a great burden of shame. He no longer passed back and forth among his tribemates. He stayed in his house much of the time. Then news spread that he was ill. My fathers, working with the tribal medicine man, worked with all their strength to heal him. But for one moon following another, his body kept wasting away. Then one night his wife Ndaya dreamed that a crocodile was trying to devour her. Everyone knows that this dream means that great sorrow is about to catch you. On the following day when the sun no longer blinds the eyes, my father's brother Beya died.

As is the custom, people gathered at Ndaya's house to mourn with her. The body was buried the following day; but the mourning continued. Relatives of both Ndaya and Beya ate and slept at Ndaya's house for two weeks. This is a debt they must fulfill. If a relative fails to come, or if he fails to join with his heart in the weeping, people will say he wanted the person to die; he may have helped the person to die. They sit around the bereaved one close as beard whiskers; then they weave slowly back and forth as if blown by the wind, creating a mourning song which recalls the good deeds of the dead one, and asking why the spirits have taken him. Ndaya listened to their singing; as oil assuages a hurting wound, her heart was comforted.

Death is the domain of the spirits. Only they can explain it. Father and his remaining brothers went to the diviner to learn who caused the death of Beya. The diviner accepted his fee of a goat, then consulted the ancestral spirits. They said no one living was guilty. They had taken his life to complete justice. "In his heart Beya kept accusing Ndaya of unfaithfulness," he said. "He accused her falsely. He did not respect the judgement of his superiors. In anger, he blackened the name of a tribemate and scarred his flesh. He who hardens his heart in the path of evil must pay its wages." Father and his brothers sadly agreed. It did not bother them to think that Beya was cursed by the spirits. This explained for them why he suffered calamaties, one hooked onto another. They would shrug a shoulder and say, "He was as a bird who breaks every twig it lights on."

After the mourning, it was the duty of Father's younger sister, Meta, to pass the nights with Ndaya. They did not sleep in the house of Beya; they slept in the kitchen hut beside it. Father was the eldest of the brothers. Early one morning Meta came, and asked to talk with Father alone.

"A spirit is troubling Ndaya. If we find no way to overpower it, I fear it will catch her, as the spirits caught Beya."

"Why do you speak thus?"

"For five nights following one another, the spirit of Beya has come to torment her in a dream. He says he will not let her go until she joins him. Last night she could not sleep for fear. This morning she is ill."

Father called my mother. With Meta they went to the kitchen hut. Ndaya, with the mourning cloth still about her waist, lay quietly on a woven mat on the ground. Her face was wet with weeping. Her eyes were closed. She did not want to talk. Meta and Mother brought her to our house. Father went to consult with his brothers. He returned, caught two white chickens, put them into a carrying basket, and waited.

Later that morning Father's brothers and the sorcerer arrived. Carrying the chickens, they all went to the house of Beya. The men stood outside the house entryway. The sorcerer took the chickens and went inside the house. Soon they heard him cry out loudly with a voice sharp and hard as a knife blade:

> "Get out of this house!
> Get out at one time with this chicken!
> May the evil that is tormenting this house leave with you!
> Go with it into the high grass of the prairie!
> Wander with it in the wilderness forever!"

Then he left the house, carrying a living white chicken. He followed the footpath down the slope into the valley until the high grass swallowed him. After awhile he appeared again, returning empty-handed.

He entered the house. The men came and squatted on the ground outside the doorway to watch. He was sitting inside the threshold, looking out. In one hand he held a small bushy branch. In the other he held the second chicken. He looked through the doorway into the sky and said:

> "Eldest of all spirits; Maker of iron.
> You whose rays burn men's eyes.
> We start no new affair;
> We follow the footsteps of our forefathers
> whose spirits You rule.
> You see us here with this fowl;
> this clean offering we bring You.
> We sprinkle its blood on this threshold.
> We drain its life onto the ground.
> Let it purify this house of evil.
> Let no evil spirit enter its doorway.
> May your curse strike any who tries.

"Shall it be thus?" he asked the men.

"Let it be thus," they answered as one.

He took a small knife from under his waist cord; he cut off

the chicken's head. He drained some of its blood onto the branch and sprinkled it onto the threshold. He drained the rest of the blood onto the ground on either side of it.

The spirit of Beya troubled Ndaya no more. She recovered. As is the duty of the eldest brother, Father took Ndaya as his wife.

Some used to say that an inherited wife is as worthless as straw baggage. Others said one should multiply wives, and thus multiply honor. When Father accepted Ndaya to be his wife, neither of these things was in his heart. He would provide her a hut, food and clothing; thus she would not need to sell her body to other men to gain the things of life. He would perform the duty given him by his forefathers; to bear children in the place of his dead brother, and thus replenish the tribe.

To take a young wife was not to shame your old one. "Never despise the wife of your youth," the elders say. "You and she have minds of the same length, because you matured together." The coming of a second wife promotes the first one to honor.

The first wife is given a name which establishes her as chief of the compound; others living in it cannot dispute her authority; they serve her.

She keeps her place in the large living-house, with her husband; the chest containing his personal things must stay in their sleeping room; the second wife lives in a hut of her own, nearby.

The first wife gets the best portion of game meat her husband brings from the forest: a thigh. Only she can prepare for him the food he needs to carry out ancestral rites. Only she can go with him to choose the place for a new house or a new field.

Thus a new hut was built near our living-house. Ndaya submitted herself to the rules of the compound, and sat in peace. Only one thing remained to make her joy sufficient.

Father tied his heart to the matter of unlocking her powers of birth. His brothers helped him gather the payment price, and the tribal medicine man made his strongest medicine. The spirits heard, and Ndaya was found to be pregnant. She rejoiced exceedingly. The burden of shame for her barrenness was being lifted. Weeks ahead of the birth, Father and his brothers began planning a day of joy which befitted such an affair.

When the time for birth was sufficient, an old woman friend stayed in Ndaya's hut to help her. Ndaya bore a baby girl. As was the custom, she stayed in the hut to fulfill eight days of purification. During those days Father could not go in to see her or his child. He prepared things for a feast on the ninth day. He hired workmen. They brought long forked sticks from the forest. In the open space next to our compound they planted the sticks in rows in the ground. Through the forks they laid bamboo poles. Upon the poles they laid freshly-cut palm fronds to make a great flat shade roof. This would be the feasting house.

The ninth day arrived. When the sun came up, it found people already working. Ndaya went to the stream to bathe, and returned, few noticing her. Women brought to our house bundles of firewood, baskets of flour, fresh greens, cooking pots, and stirring paddles. The feast would need much meat. Men butchered many of our goats and pigs. As was the custom, we all wanted to share. I gave them my goat, and strengthened my heart like a man when they killed it.

Men kept bringing large heavy yellow drinking gourds. The row of gourds on the ground beneath one edge of the shade kept growing until there were ten. They were filled with palm wine. Its fermentation slowly burbled white foam from the gourd necks and filled the air with a pungent odor which burned our nostrils. Musicians came. Drummers began a small bonfire for heat to tighten their skin drum heads. Two marimba players began arranging thin tone boards of different lengths. Each board was fastened across the top of a long slender hollow gourd which made its sound loud and rich. Then rubber hammering sticks were laid on the ground beside them.

Before the sun was hot, all was ready. People had multiplied like maggots on meat. Father stood about twenty steps from Ndaya's hut door; all gathered around to watch. In a short time Ndaya's old woman helper came out of the door carrying an empty water gourd. She dropped it to the ground and with her foot, crushed it. She picked up the pieces and threw them into a nearby waste pit. She returned into the hut. Then she brought out dirty wilted food-carrying leaves, crumpled them in her hands, and threw them in the waste pit. These are the things Ndaya used to eat and drink with during her days of confinement. Destroying them showed that the purification rites were finished.

The old woman disappeared into the hut. Then through the door came Ndaya. Her baby was in her arms. She stood and looked at the waiting people. Her joy had turned her face into that of another person. Upon seeing her, the people together, each answering his own heart, made a great roaring noise that wanted to break the sky. Then all was quiet.

Ndaya came toward Father. She placed the baby in his arms. Father looked at it for a long time, tears beginning to fall upon it. Then he had them place in Ndaya's arms two gifts: a new piece of bright-colored dress cloth, and a large red rooster. She looked at Father, tears trickling down her cheeks. Then suddenly there were many tears, no one having shame.

Three old ladies with palm fronds in their hands raised a long piercing cry, breaking it by patting their fingers to their lips. They stooped over low and swept the ground at Ndaya's feet with the fronds, as if welcoming a chief. Other older women, circling her, began singing a song, clapping their hands, twisting their hips, and stamping their right feet in rhythm. The drummers catching the sound, began a booming cadence that made every hip joint want to dance. The marimbas joined with a melody. Like one sweep of a broom, everybody was caught at once with joy, and loosed their hearts to dance.

A workman, being instructed by Father, asked us to get baskets and hoes to help him. We went to Ndaya's hut. We cleaned out the old cooking fire ashes and threw away the worn sleeping mat. We carried fresh damp earth in our baskets and dumped it onto the floor. We pushed it into the hut corners with our toes. Then we began packing it, stamping our feet and twisting our bodies in rhythm with the big people dancing outside. This was a day for all hearts to sing. We replaced Ndaya's cooking-pot stones, placed two gourds of fresh water in one corner, and laid a new sleeping mat along the wall.

When the sun was high, dancing stopped. Father had three big chairs placed at one end of the feasting shelter. He sat in the center, Mother on his right, and Ndaya, with her baby, on his left. Women carried in open-topped gourds full of steaming food. As was our custom, people squatted on the ground under the shade and ate and drank. Women came, one after another, and spoke words of comfort to Ndaya.

"The Great Elder Spirit never sleeps," they said. "In the end He justifies the innocent. He has vindicated you for your faithfulness. May He give you an abundance of children." After eating, people again danced. They continued into the night until sleep caught them standing.

Ndaya named her baby "Banseke," which means, "Let them laugh at me."

Customs like these sustained the life of my tribe. They were as familiar waters in which my people bathed daily, never querying about their source. These customs, as the strong fingers of a potter, worked to shape me into the person I was to be.

Praise Goes to My Head 7

The broad stream of water, which was my tribal life, kept flowing past me slowly year after year, without changing. But outside our small tribe, life was changing rapidly. At the end of dry season, rains come. They always change the face of the jungle, and change the streams which flow through it. White men had come. They brought with them their wisdom; some of it was good; some of it was bad. Their wisdom was changing the face of our country; and I knew that with the passing of time, it would change life in our tribes.

By the time I was born, white men had established themselves as chiefs in our country. They had driven out slave raiders and brought an end to fighting between the tribes. When peace between tribes was established, white traders came. They brought new kinds of salt and soap; soft bright-colored cloth; eating dishes made of iron instead of clay; bright lamps which chased darkness from even the corners of our house rooms; and bicycles which could eat up long journeys, the legs not wearying.

Other white people came, bringing us their healing medicines and book wisdom. Some of them wanted to teach us matters of their Great Elder Spirit. We did not understand why we needed to learn more about Him; and we had ways of dealing with many of our sicknesses. But the wisest among us had never made a paper page talk. About the reading of a book, we knew nothing.

Thus, people from the outside brought us new ideas and new customs. Little by little, they placed before our eyes a manner of living we had never known. To gather things one wants for his happiness, these people did not rely upon the kindness of their tribal fathers; each one worked for himself, earned money, and bought the things he wanted. Youth from among us who finished book-reading classes were given new kinds of work; they earned money, and gathered to themselves the white man's things in abundance.

I respected my tribal life. The love of my parents and tribesmen comforted me; their support strengthened me. But I saw what was happening around us. These things were changing the customs of our tribal life. I had a good mind. I had a body larger and stronger than most youths my age. Father had taught me how to work. Did not the name he had given me mean "the all-powerful one"? When others my age used both their minds and their bodies, earned money, and enjoyed new things in abundance, why should I be happy to remain forever in the field with a hoe? The ground squirrel, in hunting for food every day, gets accustomed to his own tiny trail. But what if one day he discovers that someone has been disturbing it? And what if, at that one time, he sees fresh berries waiting for him along a new trail?

I did not tell my father that I wanted to separate myself from our tribal way of life; I did not want him to feel I thought it was inadequate. I asked him if I could go to school. He accepted.

"I want you to progress," he said.

I entered class in a village near us. The teacher was a black man hired by the mission. I studied two years. When they saw how well I was learning, they called me to the mission station. There I studied three months, and followed their ritual known as "baptism." I did not truly give my heart to this matter; many boys my age were following the baptism custom; it was a symbol which would win favor with those who could help us progress. When I returned to begin studying at the village school the third year, the teacher told me that those over him said I was too old to study in class; they needed space for younger students; I was mature enough to start supporting myself by working in the cotton fields.

I worked in the cotton fields two years. During that time my mother became very ill. I called the mission teacher; he baptized her before she died. Then I worked one year with those who fix the iron path used by trains. I did not refuse to work with my body in the hot sun. But my studying in class had given me thirst to use my mind. There was no place any more for me to find this kind of work in the land of my ancestors. For me to realize this hope, it would be necessary for me to go to the city. When I told Father, he did not accept readily.

"I am afraid that such a path would separate you forever from our tribe."

"I could never finish my debt to my tribe," I replied. "It is only the journey that will separate me from you. All I know about life on this earth, I've learned from our people. What kind of affair could ever cut me off from them?"

"Let me show you my heart. You see how I have given you the work of feeding strangers and welcoming guests. When I am on journey, you carry the burden of the family. Someday you will take my place as chief of our clan. It is no secret that you are my favorite son. There is none whom I hope for more than for you. The elders say that even a swamp rat remembers its nest. Some people do not. They leave home forever, renounce their upbringing, and thus bring shame upon their forebears."

"Father, how could I ever be unfaithful to my upbringing? I will never forget you or my people. I beg of you; allow me to fulfill my hopes."

He looked at me hard, pondering. Then he said, "As your heart yearns, so let it be. You have always been a child who keeps his vows."

It was 1938 when I arrived at Kolwezi. I was about 18. It was the first time my eyes saw a big city with tall houses made by the white man. I found work in the copper mining company. I lived with other single men in a brick house in the work camp. We workmen were more than a thousand. We had come from all parts of our country. No one cared about my tribal origin or my home village affairs. I progressed equally with everyone.

The company was building camps of houses for its workers, and big houses here and there for its white overseers. At first I worked with a group of men under a white foreman building houses; then I learned to take care of the machines that made the fire that flows in wires they called "electricity." In the first days I learned what the white man desired; I learned what to say, and how to walk, and where not to go. I saw what happened to those who broke his laws, as I've already related to you. Each day with its little affairs followed another until four years had passed. I kept trying to guard myself well. Then came the day that my anger flashed out, and I discarded the white man.

After this happened, I kept asking myself, "Why did you do it?" At that time all I understood was that the white man was shaming me, and anger seized me. But the passing of years has helped me organize my thinking so that now I think I understand. In the copper mine company, I wanted to be somebody. I wanted to be recognized. I craved for some sign of change, that I was learning and growing, and coming to be a person of value.

I had seen it in my tribal life. There everyone was somebody. When a person's need became evident, his tribemates worked together to meet it. When his gift became evident, they arranged a way for him to make use of it. When he progressed well, they commended him. I saw this truth in the life of my father. He with his wives had worked hard and had obeyed the tribal laws for years. It was not for nothing: he had been given a name which showed his accomplishments; he was made the official guest greeter for all important occasions; he was elected chief of the clan. Because of his hard work and faithfulness, those over him had come to respect and honor him.

But now consider the new ideas and customs which kept wanting to invade our tribal life. It appeared that people who brought these ideas always wanted to humiliate us. They wanted to wipe out our value. Thus was the case with Ngongo Lutete. Thus was the case with my work of learning white man's wisdom in the village class, when I had to quit. But far surpassing these matters, it was the case in the mining company.

In this place we had worked hard and obeyed laws. To receive what? We always danced to the same song, as its players desired. We were like trained animals with hearts that did not feel, which received recompense for their obedience. We lived inside a box with the lid locked. While our faces smiled, our insides boiled with bitterness. A proverb says, "The chamaeleon is a coward; it always changes its color." How could we ever be people with our own value when we had to always wear a color that pleased those over us? Must we forever live like cowards without a word? When you are inside a closed box, if too much time passes, you suffocate. There must be some change, or you will die.

These forces were invading our country. I could not return into the womb of my tribal life and escape them; I had to face them. My upbringing would not allow them to take away my human worth and make me live as a hypocrite. If I could not be accepted in my world, the only other path left for me was to fight to change it. Thus my anger flashed out at the white man to make something change. I did not know what would happen. But even if it made him change my nickname from "baboon" today to "gorilla" tomorrow, that would be a sign of change.

It did far more than I had hoped. It brought an end to white men's offending me. It turned everything upside-down. I did something that no one else had ever done, and immediately I gained all the workers' respect. At once, I was somebody important. I had never been given such recognition even in my home village. All the workmen gathered behind me as one. They expected me to be their path cutter toward lifting their burden of shame. They also trusted me as their strength and protection if violence broke out. For the first time in their lives, they had the hope of change. They had a leader to follow. They would give me anything I wanted. So long as they supported me, I would not have to trouble my mind about anything for as long as I lived.. When I tasted this kind of recognition, I wouldn't give it up no matter what happened.

I found more than what I had expected. And I must also tell you that because of it, pride began to blind me. It made me forget many lessons of my childhood. I thought this path would lead me out into the light; but instead, it led me into great darkness. With much sorrow, I now retrace this path for others to see. If you feel with me the burden I carried in my darkness, you will share with me my joy when I find the light.

Drinking makes a person feel strong and bold. For many oppressed people, it is the one thing they can do that makes them feel like they are important. One evening we were drinking at the bar. My friends were singing a song:

"Maweja Mazungu, crusher of the white man,
You cut the path ahead of us.
You conquer in our name.
You have subdued his offending.
You have made him listen.
We thank you!
We glorify you!"

"Why not prepare a drink offering to our chief?" cried one.

"Yes! Table boy! Bring bottles of your best strong wine. Fill this table full of them. Help us prepare a gift befitting our champion, Maweja Mazungu!"

We drank. We laughed. We raised our voices, throwing words at one another.

"Meta," Kabeya called to a woman at the bar. "Come here. Maweja, there is no woman who exceeds Meta in beauty. Look at her. She knows how to make happy the heart of a man. I have known her for years. Meta, this is our chief. Sit down beside him. Give him the happiness he deserves."

My heart no longer felt the burdens of earth. My childhood years were dim and far away. The words of Meta were smooth as oil. Her hand pressed mine. My blood ran hot. When I finished what was in my drinking glass, she got up from her chair, and led me away.

52

I Kill a Soldier 8

There were two things that I desired above all else: to show the white man that I was equal with him; and to fulfill the expectations of my worshippers so that they would continue to support me. I had already learned that if a person shows his bravery by doing something no one else has done, people will honor him. I figured out in my thinking something I could do which no one else had ever done, and which would also show my equality with my superiors. I would imitate the white man. If I did all the things he did, in the end he would have to accept that I was his equal; and at the same time, my followers would support me with hearts of fire.

And so, like the white man, I began to go where I chose. I drank what I wanted and as much as I wanted. I began to smoke; as I'd seen with many white men, a stick of tobacco hung from my mouth most of the time. I refused to cut my hair. I bought medicine that, rubbed into it, would straighten it, like a white man's. It grew to stand out almost the width of my shoulders. I dressed like the white man. I bought hard-bottomed shoes with pieces of iron on their heels. I wore them to work. I clacked them loudly when walking, strutting like a white chief. When talking with others, I placed my hands on my hips. In a few weeks, everybody knew me. My friends smiled with admiration; white people gnashed their teeth with contempt.

53

Sometimes when I lay awake at night, my mind wanted to argue with my heart. "Where will this matter end? Do you really feel you will become one in tallness with the white man? You may as well try cutting a tree trunk with your teeth. Where are the teachings of your childhood? Don't you remember the proverb: 'A long-tailed animal should never try to jump across a fire'? If you don't quit this path, what your heart covets most will be the death of you."

But I knew the white man's thinking about us was false. Why should I be content for men to have faith in falsehood, and thereby find happiness in tormenting us and our progeny forever? I was exposing their twisted thinking. I might compel some to abandon it. I owed a debt not only to my tribe, but to my race. If I laid down my life for this, would it be for nothing? And so pride, like a boa constrictor, allured me by its beauty, and began to wrap me tightly.

One day I was looking for something new to do. I drank too much and became insolent. I went to church to take Holy Communion. My only desire in doing this was to mock the priest who was a white man, and to show arrogance that would catch the eyes of people watching me. I sat on the steps in front of the church waiting. People entered. The priest preached his words, me listening. Then he called people to come kneel at the altar to receive the Holy Food. At that time I rose, entered the church, and walked its length, striking my hard shoes on the floor, shaking my hair, and strutting like a white chief. I knelt at the altar with the others, closed my eyes, opened my mouth, and received the Holy Food.

For some weeks, this custom of mine startled my followers. Then the time came for me to do something new. Once upon leaving the church from taking Communion, I asked my friends to follow me. We returned to the work camp and went to the house of a woman who made wine of fire to sell to the people. Only one cup of it, and I was drunk. My friends, eight young men and two young women, sat around the long table. I bought a fried pastry and a large cup of fire wine. I stood at the head of the table.

"Do you want to have the strength of Maweja Mazungu?" I

asked them, holding the pastry in my hand. "Eat this, each of you; it is my body."

I passed to them the pastry. Each of them broke off a piece and ate it.

"Do you want the courage of Maweja Mazungu?" I asked, holding the wine cup in my hand. "Drink this, each of you; it is my blood. I'm not going to be with you much longer. The day is coming when you will see me return in the clouds of the sky."

These words were stupid. In a manner I was not expecting, some of them were fulfilled very soon.

We finished our meeting about three o'clock in the afternoon. My legs led me to the house of a harlot I preferred above others. She saw me approaching. Her face frowned with disgust.

"Maweja, why are you drunk again? Scolding you has wearied me. Have you not yet understood that wine makes you become like an animal?"

"I will do what my heart desires. Is it your affair?"

"If you want to call me your woman, it is my affair. I will not have you. I loathe you."

Anger began burning like fire.

"You say you loathe me? You say you will not have me? No, it is not thus. You will do what I say."

I seized her. She resisted. We fought. She tore my shirt. I released her.

"You, a woman, have torn my clothes. For this I will not kill you. I will only maim you. I will break your arm. Then, even if you flee me, you will always look at your crooked arm and remember, 'That's what I got for refusing Maweja Mazungu.'"

She fastened her eyes to me until she understood that I was not lying. Fear caught her. She screamed. She ran into her house and locked the door. I pounded the door with my fists. It was iron and would not open. I ran around to one side of the house to a wooden window. I struck it and smashed it. When the woman saw this she opened the door and fled. When I returned to the front of the house, she was gone.

People were coming from everywhere to learn what the noise was about. They were telling one another, "This man has gone crazy. He's starting a fight." Then a white man arrived in a car. He was the overseer of the workmen's camp. He got out, put his hands on his hips, and watched me. He did not touch me.

"Because you wanted to start a fight in my camp, would you get into the car? We will go see the government man."

I did not refuse. I told myself that if where we were going they wanted to harm me, I would fight them.

We went to the house of the white Belgian government man, who was Chief of Police. We got out of the car, went and stood on the veranda. The overseer told him about me. Then he gave an order.

"Police, take this man to prison. Let him stay there tonight. We will look into his affair tomorrow."

They came and circled around me. They looked at me from my hair to my shoes, then at my face. They did not touch me.

"Let's go," I said. "I'll follow you to prison."

The prison was a high fence made of brown bricks. Its sides were longer than its opposite ends. They opened the big door on its end; I entered; they closed the door. Against the long wall on either side was a row of rooms, covered with a narrow roof. Black soldiers were doing the work of prison guards. I saw some of them bringing ropes. A sergeant cried out.

"Tie him!"

"Don't touch me. Before you tie me, I'll kill twenty of you; if need be, I'll die with number twenty-one."

They watched me, stepping this way and that, as if plotting to seize a cornered lion. I was trapped. A power seized me that I could not master. I wanted to warn them of my feelings inside. I saw a wooden door near me. I struck the door hard with my fist, and split it.

"Be careful with that man," one soldier said. "See how anger has inflamed his eyes? We'd better not touch him now."

"That one person is stronger than this many men?" cried the sergeant. "Tie him up."

"Let no hand touch me," I warned.

They slowly moved toward me. My anger would not be restrained. Heat shot into my arms and fingers. I saw a wooden

56

axe handle at my feet. I seized it, raised it high, struck a solider, crushed his skull, and killed him. It was July 1, 1944. On that day, as a child tosses a twig into a rushing river, my deed threw me into torment.

I am Beaten, Bound

Soldier-guards fled from the prison. They cried out, "He killed a man!" I bounded through the open door, as a lion from its cage. I threw myself into a screaming mob. I fought with all my strength to make a path through it, but failed. I was thrown to the ground. Dust choked and blinded me. They beat me; women; other prisoners; soldiers. They beat me with sticks, fists and feet. When you have killed a soldier, who will have mercy?

"Cut off his head!" cried the sergeant. The people answered with a roar. Blows like hammers hit me everywhere.

"Don't kill him! Make room! The person killing him will be judged in his place. Tie him up." It was the voice of the Belgian Chief of Police.

The beating stopped. Soldiers rolled me onto my stomach. They tied my wrists behind me. Then they wrapped a rope around my upper arms, pulling it tight until my elbows touched together and my arm bones felt pulled out of my shoulders. I was made to stand on my feet. I was pushed inside the prison to a heavy door. There I was thrown to the ground. They tied my ankles, then pulled them up behind me to my wrists and tied them. I was bent backwards into a round tight bundle. They opened the heavy door, another door inside it, pushed me into darkness, and closed them. After a short time the doors opened; I was soaked with two buckets of water; the doors closed again. Then all was silent.

My face was swelling from the beating, but my eyes could see. My cell was small, about three by six feet, with walls about twelve feet high. Its floor was concrete; it had no ceiling. Its only light came through a narrow space between the roof and the top of the outside wall. Its air was stale. It was bare.

My body was sore. Tied thus, whenever I moved, I suffered. Light over the edge of the wall faded; I knew night had come. With it came the beginning of suffering I did not know existed upon earth. My soaked rope bonds began to shrink. Slowly they pulled themselves into my flesh. Then came thirst.

I was as a captured lion. Once I was lord of everyone; I had flattered or terrorized people, as it pleased me. Now that I was locked in a box, my rage boiled. It boiled most fiercely toward those who were causing my suffering. Perhaps this was good. Because my mind was working with rage, it was not broken with pain.

A long time passed. Light began to appear over the wall. Then the outside door opened. On the inside door was a square hole through which things could be passed. An arm holding a tin can reached through the hole toward me. With great pain I rolled onto my stomach. I stretched my head to reach it. My thirst made the cup as big as my head. With all my strength, I got my lips about two inches from the cup, but no closer. It seemed the arm was tormenting me; I cursed my pain, my helplessness, the owner of that arm. Then it stretched itself toward me. The cup touched my lips, and tipped. The water was foul-tasting. It could be poisoned. But it was cool. It answered the cry of thirst. I drank it.

Light and darkness over the wall showed me the passing of three days. Each day brought with it greater suffering. I ate no food. I drank bad-tasting water from the tin can. Because of the way my body was tied, it could not relieve itself. Meat cut by the bonds on my arms and ankles was rotting; its foul odor filled the cell and restrained my breathing. The darkness of no-moon night wrapped itself tightly around my thinking.

Then something happened which should have turned me

59

around. Once, while lying quietly in the darkness of my box, I saw a pure-white person looking down at me. A brightness circled his neck like a collar, and lightened his face. After looking upon me for a time, he disappeared. In a short time he returned a second time, then a third time. Then he disappeared, and did not return. I was so filled with the darkness of my evil that the vision meant nothing to me; it left only a small footprint on my memory.

On the fourth day my cell door opened. My ankle bonds were cut and I was lifted to my feet. I went out and looked at myself. Flesh along my ankle wounds was putrefied, and my feet were exceedingly swollen. By moving my fingers behind me, I knew that my hands and wrist wounds were the same.

The Chief of Police prepared travel papers. Soldiers brought an iron collar. It was made of a heavy rod, and hinged at the back, its ends bent to make two eyes to receive a padlock at its front. They passed one eye through the end link of a heavy chain about nine-feet long. They closed the collar around my neck and locked it. Four soldiers with guns walked me to the train station. The chain dragged itself behind me, making its noise, people looking at me. My guards put me into a boxcar, laid me on its floor, and retied my ankles, the bonds falling again into their place. They closed the door, and sat down around me. The train jerked. It was night. I began a journey of ten hours from Kolwezi to the city of Likasi for judgment.

At that time my mind had no place for pondering my dilemma. Since that time my mind has often explained it to me by a fable.

The chief of the forest had two daughters. One of them was courted by an elephant; the other was courted by a frog. The frog was greatly humiliated by his small size. He devised wisdom by which he might have honor which exceeded that of the elephant.

One day he said to his girlfriend, "You may think that because I am small, I am worthless. But don't be deceived by my size. In fact, I am more important than that elephant."

"Truly?" marvelled the girl. "But how can we know it unless you show us?"

60

"I have never told you," answered the frog, "but I customarily use the elephant as my horse. The day is coming when you will see it with your own eyes."

The next day the elephant came. The girls told him the words of the frog. The elephant was furious. He went to the home of the frog.

"Who do you think you are, telling the girls such words?" he asked.

"What did the girls tell you I said?"

"You told them that you are more important than I."

"Honorable elephant, how could I, a tiny frog, say that about one as great as you? Don't you perceive what the girls are trying to do? They are trying to destroy our friendship by making us jealous of each other. Let us not be tricked by their cleverness."

"It is true that we have been friends for a long time. But how can I determine who is telling the truth?"

"Let the girls' friendship be broken, but let ours remain," said the frog. "Let us go together to see them, and settle the matter."

The elephant accepted with joy.

The journey was long. The frog hopped slowly to make it longer. The elephant became impatient and cross.

"Can't you travel any faster? Night will catch us."

"Hopping without resting makes me very weary," the frog replied. "The speed of your journey is one with your greatness. I have no weight. If you want to arrive quickly and we are friends, why don't you let me hop onto your back?"

The elephant agreed. He now walked rapidly. Only forest flies buzzing around his head distracted him. From time to time he stopped to shake his head and to chase them with his trunk.

"Honorable elephant, why should flies impede your journey? I can help you. Just break a twig off the tree and give it to me; I'll chase them away."

This the elephant did.

Thus when the girls saw the frog riding the elephant with a

switch in his hand, they agreed that he used the elephant for his horse.

Two frogs had mounted themselves upon my back: pride and anger. Without my understanding it, they had driven me to drunkenness, fornication, and now to murder. Once I thought they were my friends.

I had been tricked. They were my masters.

My Death Sentence 10

We arrived at Likasi when people were beginning to stir from their sleep. My guards untied my feet and walked me to prison. It was like the last prison, only much larger. They stripped off my clothing and put on me a pair of short black pants. They shaved my head. They untied my wrists, then retied them in front of me so that I could work at feeding myself. I looked at my arms; my stomach twisted. The wrist bonds had almost buried themselves in rotting flesh. The skin on my hands and fingers was blue, and wanted to split.

Guards fastened my ankles in bands of iron connected with a short chain. My neck iron remained. They locked me into a cell with five other men. Because of the odor from my wounds, those with me loathed me. Days of waiting passed. More and more my mind began to grasp my plight; I feared what was to come, and had no hope of changing it. I was lost in a cavern of empty blackness. Every offense of a soldier-guard pushed me deeper into the dark. How was I yet to suffer? Who would ever show me a way of escape? What would be my end?

On the morning of the tenth day, two black soldiers with guns walked me out of the prison to the tribunal building, and made me to stand before a judge. He was a white man. He sat behind a large table with papers spread out before him. Black helpers sat on either side of him. This man would decide my sentence. His eyes followed slowly from my head to my feet, his mind taking a careful picture of me. The odor of rotting flesh was always with me.

"Where does this man come from?" he asked sharply.

"From prison," a soldier replied.

"How long has he been there?"

"We do not know."

"When did you enter prison?" he asked me.

"Ten days ago."

"When you arrived, were you shown to the director of the prison?"

"No."

He looked angrily at the soldiers.

"Your work at prison is to guard people. Look at this man. Do you feel that you have done your work well? Has it been your mind to guard him, or to kill him?"

His words were like the light of a match, wanting to call me. He ordered a sick-bed truck. It took me to a hospital. They untied my wrists; my neck and leg irons remained. They treated my rope wounds, a soldier with a gun standing at my bedside. At the end of two months the wounds were healing. I was taken to the judge again. I hoped much that he might help me.

"We have received your papers from Kolwezi where you were arrested," he said. "For many years you were a good worker in the copper mining company. What changed your heart, so that this trouble has caught you?"

My mind was not able to find the answer to such a question. It was still busy plotting acts of vengeance against those who tormented me. My words were as arrows shot by a blind man.

"Ask those who caught me. I had broken no laws. I had harmed no one."

"Then why did you kill a soldier?"

"I was following my own affairs; soldiers came with ropes to tie me."

His eyes wanted to bore into me like red-hot nails.

"It is clear that you have not yet thought carefully about your trouble. They will take you back to prison. I will see you again."

64

The match-light went out. My blackness returned. I was delivered again into the hands of my tormentors.

Soldiers took me to prison. They laid me stomach-down on the ground in the middle open area. They lowered my pants. They brought a mfimbu whip. They lashed me eight times across the buttocks. Then they returned me to my cell. They whipped me thus every morning. They were doing this for two reasons: to avenge the death of their comrade, and to teach me that it was foolish to rebel against their authority. By the tenth day flesh on my buttocks was shredded. My hips were sore. They let me rest a few days. Then the judge called for me. I walked with suffering.

Again, by asking questions, he tried to uncover the reasons which brought me trouble. Because of my suffering, my mind had no room for new thoughts. He was about to return me to prison when I spoke.

"Sir, don't you see my condition? By now the mfimbu has shredded my buttocks. The poison of my wounds has filled my body. Will you send me back to prison to rot? Why don't you kill me?"

"Why have you been whipping him?" he asked my guards.

"Because he tried to escape," they lied.

He sent me to a dispensary nearby. They laid me on a bed and left. Then I heard my soldier-guard talk with the girl-nurse who was to care for me.

"That man is dangerous. He should not have mercy. If you want to make us happy, when you clean his wounds, cut them back so they bleed well."

My arm wounds had begun to dry. Who was a girl to despise the word of a soldier with a gun? That night, with the soldier watching, she opened my wounds again. She pulled the skin and cut with a scissors into the living flesh around my arm. Much blood flowed. She filled the wounds with salve-medicine. The next morning they were swollen and hurting. I knew this was death. I longed for it. Then they pushed me into my cell and locked the door.

The next morning no one came to take me out for a beating. Nor the morning which followed. For days following one after another, I was counted as one with the other prisoners in my cell. We were given no work to do; we were all waiting sentence. Two more months passed. From time to time the white judge called me to ask more questions. They passed off me like raindrops off a banana leaf. The light did not flicker again. When the judge talked to me the last time, my last hope disappeared.

"I have tried to send your thinking in the right path," he said. "I wanted to help you accept the evil of what you have done, and to understand what pushed you to do it. I saw this as the only way out of your trouble. But you have closed your mind against it. Thus I have no power to help you. We are sending you to the provincial tribunal at the capital city of Lubumbashi. There they will review our decision. I must ask that they sentence you to prison for life."

I was sent to Lubumbashi. It was January of 1945. They put me into a hospital. They tested my blood, and spinal water, and other things; they wanted to know if my anger-sickness came from insanity. Then I waited two months in a sentencing cell in prison. Then the word came:

"We change nothing. Whenever you die, on that day your prison term will be finished."

I Hide My Evil ▌▌

As was true of all centers of authority at that time, the prison was in the hands of Belgians. Its soldier-guards were of my own race. It will be my home for a large part of my story. So I must help you fix its picture clearly in your mind.

I had never seen so large a prison. Its walls were of brown brick; the cement on their top edges was full of broken glass. They enclosed a space sufficient for more than one thousand prisoners.

The prison entryway was a large door in the middle of an end wall. When you enter, a wide path of gravel leads your eye straight ahead to a tall viewing-tower in the center of the prison compound. Standing high inside the tower is a soldier with his gun, watching. Buildings are arranged along the entry-path and around the tower.

First, on the left side of the path is the prison office building where secretaries work, and where our records are kept; in its far inside wall, a door leads you into the office of the white prison director. Following the office building is the medical clinic. Next on your left hand as you move toward the tower, is a building with cells for white prisoners.

On the right-hand side of the entry-path and opposite the prison office is a large kitchen-building where food is cooked for the prisoners. Following it is a large open space covered smoothly with gravel. Next, across from the building for white prisoners, is a large storehouse guarding food, garments, and work tools sufficient for this number of prisoners.

Having passed these buildings upon our left and right, we see five narrow buildings arranged like the spokes of a wheel; each starts from near the tower at the center, and points toward the outside wall. In them prisoners sleep. The first begins near the tower and reaches straight from our left hand toward the left wall. Following it are four others. The last one begins near the tower and reaches straight toward the right wall; building spokes sufficient to make half a wheel.

On each building-end pointing toward the tower are two small cells with locked iron-rod doors; here are kept prisoners whose conduct does not allow them to mix with others. On the inside of each sleeping-building, a wall along its length divides it into two long narrow rooms. In each room are two long rows of beds. Each bed is made like two wooden platforms, one high, one low.

Now return your mind to the picture of half a wheel. Between the last two spokes, along the outside wall to our right, is a shower building for taking baths. Near it is a water pit with a pipe and faucet for washing things. Between the next building-spokes which point toward the far corner of the prison, is a large roof covering rows of concrete tables; here we eat. The third spoke goes straight ahead of us toward the back wall. Between its end and the wall are the prison toilet pits. Beyond them a path leads through a small door in the wall to a roof-covered path; along its sides are twelve small cells with doors of a thick sheet iron, and walls thirty feet high. The prisoner in such a cell, with no food and no blanket to cover himself with at night, suffers exceedingly. I slept in the second long building from ᵗhe left, near its end toward the tower.

Each prisoner wore garments with wide stripes, yellow and blue. Trousers were long and full, with a tieing-string around the waist; the shirt was passed over the head, without front-opening. I and a few others had iron collar bands with long dragging chains; our hands and feet were not bound.

Each morning the sentry in the tower rang a bell to awaken

us. We walked in rows to the gravel-covered space between the kitchen and storehouse along the right side of the entry-path. We stood in lines for roll call. Then we went to the tables to eat large loaves of mush and perhaps meat which was prepared for us during the night. Then many of us were put into the hands of soldier-guards to go do different kinds of work.

During my first months, another prisoner and I were fastened together by our neck bands each day, and were sent outside with a soldier to hoe down high grass. While thus working under the hot sun, I had time to think; but my thinking did not lead me to good conduct. No question remained about my sentence; others had decided how to deal with my body. The problem remained how to deal with the person inside myself. This was my problem. It surpassed me. To make my life more bitter, I was now chained to the neck of another.

Is this how my grandfather had felt when his neck was tied to that of another? Perhaps. But no; his affair was different from mine. Slavery had caught him by accident; he had not earned it. With courage, he could retain a tatter of self-worth. But my slavery was different; by acts of my own choosing, I had called it upon myself. I now saw myself as a person bound three times: when working in the copper mine, I'd felt that the attitudes of those over me bound me; after that, different forms of evil enslaved me; now, civil authorities had imprisoned me. My grandfather found liberation; I would not. What was I to hope for? Nothing. So I surrendered myself to despair, not caring if I died now or later. I did whatsoever evil I felt would give me pleasure. My soldier guard became my helper in these things. He began telling himself, "This man will be in prison until he dies anyhow; why deny him all earthly happiness?"

One can see a cloth is very dirty without studying closely its spots. And so the evil I did while outside the walls I will relate with few words. I arranged with friends who came to see me, to bring me liquor and tobacco sticks. When unchained from another prisoner, I raped women who worked alone in their fields. For many days and in many ways, I had suffered at the hands of others; now I sought pleasure by causing others to suffer.

69

I was clever to hide my evil so that I would not be caught. My soldier-guard did not report me. Prison authorities thought I was behaving well. They changed my work. They needed someone with a big strong body. Food was carried in large fuel drums cut in half. They needed someone to carry meat from the market, and drums full of ball-loaves of mush to the eating tables. They removed the collar from my neck and gave me work in the kitchen.

This was hard work. After midnight we cooked. During the day we made journeys to the open-air market for fresh meat. But I liked this work. Above all, I was happy to be rid of my iron collar and its dragging chain. I did not change my manner of living. I sharpened my cleverness so as to continue my evil without my authorities hearing about it.

We went to the market for meat three times a week. I created wisdom by which I could gain authority over the kitchen foreman. He was a prisoner, but with a body smaller than mine. When he finished buying meat, I would put the largest pieces into my half-barrel and lift it onto my shoulder to carry it. This was to remind him that I was stronger than he. I did this many times. One day we arrived at the kitchen. I put my barrel to the ground in a manner that its noise showed its weight.

"My strong body helps you well, does it not?" I asked him.

"Yes, it helps me."

"When will you start repaying me?"

"Why should I repay you? Who among us has anything? We are all prisoners doing our work."

"I am not harming you. If you thought carefully about it, you would find a way to recompense me which would not increase your poverty."

"What is it you are wanting to say?"

I straightened myself and stood with my hands on my hips. "If you wanted to make me happy, when meal time comes, you would put on my plate a piece of meat which accommodates the size of my body."

Days passed. The size of my meat was no different from that of others. Then one day when returning from market, I told him to arrange this affair immediately; if not, I would use my strong body for something other than carrying a drum of meat. Beginning the next morning, and for all the mornings following, my plate had a larger piece of meat.

Things went well for awhile. Then I began to notice; at mealtime other prisoners would glance at my plate and grumble. One of them, whose name was Nkumbi, became jealous. He spoke words designed to foment ill will against me; he tried to gather a group of prisoners to accuse me to prison authorities; thus he alone would not suffer consequences.

One night after lights were out and each person was lying on his platform, Nkumbi kept allowing words of jealousy to spill from his mouth. I listened quietly. Others began speaking one mind with him. Their words gained speed like a growing whirlwind. Why should they tolerate such partiality? Then the lights came on.

"Who is making all this noise?" It was a soldier-guard.

Everyone was quiet.

"Do you think this is a public market? Who in this house does not know the strong rule against making noise at sleeping time?"

No blanket moved.

"Who among you started the talking?"

There was no answer.

"I don't want to make you all suffer. Who started this noise?"

I spoke. "It was Nkumbi."

He paused. "Is it true? You others, what do you say?"

No one spoke.

The guard went to Nkumbi's platform and pushed his body onto the floor. "Come on. Let's go outside."

We waited.

Suddenly, like a knife cutting through the night, came the slap of the mfimbu and the cries of a man in pain: one . . . two . . . three . . . four . . . five . . . six . . . then silence. Nkumbi was returned to his platform. My insides were tasting sweetness like sugar. The next day I spoke to him alone.

"I'm going to die here; it has already been decided. Whether it is now or later is of little matter to me. But unless you stop your useless talk, you'll die with me. It would be a simple

71

matter for me; to do it, I have strength, and I have tools in the kitchen."

Thus I locked his lips forever.

This is an example of how I came to be master of two domains: one was secret; my comrades said, "He rules us with terror"; the other was before the eyes of my white superiors who said, "He is carrying his responsibilities well."

The Riddle 12

It was the work of those in the kitchen to carry food to prisoners locked in small cells in the long-building ends near the tower. We carried food to them three times a day, and thus got to know them well. Some prisoners were guarded in these cells for a few weeks, being punished for some misconduct which had caught them. Other prisoners were kept in these cells forever: people who had rebelled against government authorities; those whose greatness of suffering had broken their minds; or those whose minds were always as minds of little children. One of these prisoners was different from all the others; no one disputed it. I began to fix my mind upon him.

His name was Simon Kimbangu. He lived in a cell on the end of building number three, next to the one in which I slept. His cell was about four by six feet. Along its back wall was a narrow concrete sleeping platform. Upon it were a flat reed sleeping mat and two prison blankets which, during daytime, were always neatly folded.

Kimbangu was no taller than most men. His body was somewhat heavy. Perhaps his years were twice my own. His face had begun to show the wrinkles of age. His head was balding; his hair was beginning to grey. People said he had performed healing miracles at his home village near Kinshasa, two thousand miles away, and that he and his followers had begun to threaten the authority of the colonial government. Like me, he was in prison for life. Sometimes his cell door was opened, and he walked around freely among us. At other times, when his teachings affected prisoners in a way which displeased those over us, he was locked inside his cell.

In what way was his conduct different? He refused to take any part in our jealousies, our hating each other, our secret efforts to do one another evil. He had no room in his mind for such things. When he was not locked up, every morning he would try to greet each prisoner, one by one, shaking his hand. When others persecuted him, he never showed anger toward them. He was a man of kindness, quietness and peace. He did things which we could not understand. But we respected him. Though we would not tell one another, each of us sensed that his way of acting worked to weaken the poison in our hearts.

Sometimes when we took him food, we found food from the last meal still on its plate, untouched. One time the plates of neglected food kept increasing until there were six. The kitchen overseer told me to report the matter to the prison director. The director ordered that Kimbangu be given four lashes with the mfimbu. Why did he act in a way that hunted suffering for himself? At the next meal I took him food. When time passed, I returned to see if he had eaten it. The mush was gone; the piece of meat remained. The next day I watched him do an amazing thing.

His cell door was not locked at that time. Every day, two or three hundred prisoners were sent outside to work, and would return to prison in midafternoon. On this day, when they began returning, Kimbangu stood at the entry door and began sharing his meat with each one, tiny thread by tiny thread, so that it sufficed for all of them.

It appeared the prison director did not like such conduct. Soon I saw guards going with Kimbangu to the far end of the prison. They opened the little door leading to the cells of torment, and left. The guards returned alone.

All of us had seen guards bring dead persons from these cells. Why did Kimbangu act like he did? I could not explain it. I began to fear he might die.

On the third day guards went through the door and brought Kimbangu into prison again. What was the first thing he did? He shook the hand of each of his guards, thanking them. Then he went to prisoners and guards wherever he found them, and shook their hands, greeting them. Then he entered the office of the prison director. A few of us near the kitchen moved opposite the office door to watch. There was a law which said no prisoner could touch the director. Kimbangu reached the director's desk, stood erect before him, saluted him, then turned and left.

My mind fought day and night to find a reason for such a way of acting. I began studying every piece of wisdom which I could remember from childhood to find a clue. How could a man be so different from me? To have a bigger piece of meat, I threatened people with death. Kimbangu gave all his meat away. I did all sorts of evil; when people punished me for it, I hated them and plotted vengeance. Kimbangu did no one evil. When people punished him for nothing, he showed only kindness toward them; he counted them people of worth. He had been acting in this fashion for a long time. When I learned the number of days he had been in prison, it surpassed me to believe. He had been in this place for twenty-five years. [5]

To unriddle such a path of thinking was like trying to untangle the vines of a forest. It surpassed me. I stopped trying. But I began to feel that he had something which I needed exceedingly. What was it? As an elusive animal continually evading snares, it escaped me. I would see it a bit, then lose it again. Finally, a proverb from my childhood found a path to enter my thinking; it enabled me to corner and seize the matter.

"A sheep is the king of animals," I remembered. "It does not balk or fight like a goat; it accepts with dignity whatever is forced upon it, even death."

In a few ways, Kimbangu's thinking agreed with mine. He had established that certain things were true. He gave himself to defending these truths, no one having power to change him. But beginning at this point, we differed.

The work of defending his truths caused him to respect himself. My work of defending my truths drew me into all kinds of hard affairs, and wiped out my self-respect. Why were our ends so different? It appeared that the truths we defended were different. How did they differ?

I began to see as a man walking all night begins to see a first sign of dawn. My truth said that those who helped me should be respected; but those who hindered me were to be mocked, humiliated, even destroyed. Kimbangu's truth said that all persons were of value; be they good or bad, they must be respected equally with himself. In thus respecting others, he could keep respect for himself. Even if others forced evil upon him, he would accept it with dignity.

Dignity. Was not this for what my heart craved? Perhaps. Something which would bring an end to my balking and fighting. Something which would make me, like the sheep, so quiet and strong that no abuse of men could degrade me. Something which showed everyone that I counted *myself* to be a person of value equal with all men. Where had Kimbangu found the truth that made him into such a person? Could he help me find it?

But showing friendship toward Kimbangu would ruin my reputation with prison authorities. They could punish me. If they saw me following the footsteps of Kimbangu, next time they would send both of us to the cells of torment.

But I had boasted to prisoners that I did not fear death to do them evil. Did I now fear death to do myself good? If I had lost my dignity, had I also lost my courage? When a hunter finally has a dead partridge in hand, he doesn't leave it in the crotch of a tree hoping sweat will cook it. He puts it on the fire.

I was still habitually doing evil. How would I talk with a man such as Kimbangu? One day he was passing among us, not being noticed. I wanted to appear fittingly pious, so I framed words I thought would please him.

"Why is it that we call to God, but He doesn't answer us? We worship ancestral spirits, but they don't respond?"

He looked at me quietly for a moment, then spoke.

"When you eat a bitter fruit, what does your face show?"

"It shows bitterness."

"When you eat a good-flavored sweet fruit, what does your face show?"

"It shows happiness."

"The forefathers said, 'Keep eating at the lime pit long enough, and you'll have white jaws; keep eating frog legs, and you'll break out with rash,' If you so covet evil in your heart that its bitterness shows clearly on your face, why should your Creator hear you?"

His answer cut me. It showed me that my evil ways showed themselves on my face; it showed me that God would not hear my crying until my heart wanted to forsake them.

Pages from God 13

Months passed, one following another. I continued to show my evil face toward those close to me, and my good face to those in authority over me. From time to time I would join a small group of prisoners to hear something of Kimbangu's teaching. Only after many months did my heart begin to accept it as true. I could not continue blaming those around me for my evil. The wisdom of my ancestors rebuked me: "Don't say that bad odor is because you've just eaten bean leaves; it has been with you for a long time." My problem was within myself.

What had the white judge said? "There is only one path out of your trouble: you must accept the evil you have done, and understand what pushed you to do it." By now, these forces which I could not understand had pushed me into doing all kinds of evil. They ruled me like demon spirits. Our village people used blood of a chicken sacrifice to cleanse a person from transgression of their laws; our sorcerer used it to drive out evil spirits. But me being here in prison, how would I ever find blood with power to cleanse me from my sinfulness, and to drive out my demons?

One night during my fifth year in prison, we were preparing to lie down to sleep. I noticed a new prisoner sitting quietly on his low platform with his head bowed and his eyes closed. I watched him follow this custom every night before sleeping.

My heart kept prodding me to learn why. One night while he was doing it, I walked to his platform.

"What are you doing?"

He started, looked up at me, and said, "I'm praying to my God."

"The God you have there, do you think He would take a person like me?"

"He will take the worst person on earth, even a murderer."

"Are you lying to me?"

"I am not lying. His promise says that the person who covers his sins will not prosper, but he who confesses and forsakes them will find mercy." [6]

The lights went out.

"My name is Maweja; what is yours?"

"Mutombo."

"When will you tell me more of this affair?"

"Come in good time tomorrow night; we will talk."

I pondered these things a long time before sleep finally caught me. The next evening I entered the sleeping house early to see Mutombo.

"How do you know your God will accept me?"

"In His book we read of a man named Saul. He was a champion at causing people to suffer. He had tied his heart to destroy the people of God. One day when he was on a journey doing this work, an exceedingly bright light struck him. He fell to the ground blind. Then he heard someone say, 'Saul, Saul, why are you tormenting me? I am Jesus.' What he saw and heard turned his life around. He became a champion of God, to bless people instead of tormenting them."

I did not tell him how these words affected me. Whenever my mind was not busy, they were like thorns which kept pricking me. One does not despise the bougainvillea because of its thorns; he endures its thorns to enjoy its flowers. And so I endured the pricking of these words because I felt the drawing of their goodness. As this person Saul, I tormented others. I mocked Jesus. In doing these things, was I tormenting Him? Did these words mean that, in spite of all my evil, He was willing to forgive me?

Mutombo finished his prison term and left. More months passed. Then one day I received a magazine called *News of Kasai Peoples.* It was from Mutombo. It was printed at the mission station at his home town of Luebo, in the province of Kasai. I began receiving a copy from month to month. In it person after person told how he found power from Jesus to turn his life around: a chief who had ruled with cruelty . . . a store clerk who was the slave of drink . . . a man with lust for harlots . . . . a sorcerer who had killed people with witchcraft. Often they quoted sayings which had helped them, from books whose names were strange to me. The more I read, the more my insides became parched with thirst. Then one day I met a prisoner named Kayembe. He had finished his studies at a mission station. I showed him one of the magazines.

"Have you seen one of these before?" I asked him.

"Yes. I know about that paper."

"These stories about people; are they true, or are they imagined?"

"Don't you see the addresses? Would the writer give persons' addresses if their stories were false?"

"Look at these sayings here. Where do they come from?"

"They come from the Book of God. They call it the Bible. Those names show what part of that book they come from."

"I heard about this book years ago. For a long time I've been wanting to read it. Where can I find one?"

"Here in prison they have a hard rule against reading it. Anyone caught with it is punished."

"Why?"

"Because it teaches about freedom. It tells how to become delivered from oppression. The Belgians over us do not want us to read it; they fear it will stir us up to revolt against them. Have you not heard why Kimbangu is here? That is where he got his teaching."

I swore to myself that I would lay hold onto that book.

"You have none of this book with you?"

He looked at me, not wanting to answer, wondering if he could trust me.

"I have only a few pages which I keep hidden."

"Believe me; a hard affair has caught me. Would you let me see just one page?"

He stared at me, thinking. Then he led me to one end of the sleeping room. We faced into a corner. He looked around to see that no one was watching. Then he removed from beneath his trouser belt a tiny package of folded papers. He gave me one, refolded the others, and slipped them beneath his belt. I did the same with mine.

I began reading it in secret. I lapped up its words. I craved more. I devised a plan.

I was going to the market for meat every Friday. When I went, I had the habit of meeting my friends there. They were my helpers in evil; they brought me what I needed for my pleasures. When I went the next time, two of them were waiting for me. They had a bottle of liquor. We drank. Before leaving I told them what I desired.

"When I come next time, please bring me a sheet from the Book of God."

"From what?"

"From the Book of God. They call it the Bible. Ask some missionaries; they study it."

My friends looked at each other in puzzlement, then replied, "We will try."

And so I began a new custom. Every Friday I got a new sheet from the Bible. One week I would get a sheet from a part called Matthew; another week from Luke. I did not want to keep more than four or five at a time; they would be difficult to hide. If those over me discovered what I was doing, they might learn the hypocrisy of my way of life, and all would be ruined. The fear of my iron collar and of the terror cell were always with me.

I kept reading. My one question was this: Would God take notice of me, rotten as I was, and change me into a new person like He had changed Saul? This question agitated my thinking day and night. If He would, He would break the chains of cruelty and lust and pride and anger which bound me. His doing this to me would be proof that He held me to be a person of value. And if God, in spite of all my sinfulness, put such a

81

price on me, how could I ever again doubt my own value? Perhaps this is where Kimbangu had found his self-respect. If I could seize this truth for myself, then men of earthly wisdom could put on me whatever price they desired; it would mean nothing to me. I devoured these pages; they entered into my blood and bones. I would discard older sheets in the toilet pit, and go to the market for more.

This continued for many months. From time to time a prisoner would catch me reading. Many of them were seeking means of taking vengeance on me. Perhaps they thought I was looking at any useless piece of paper. Perhaps they had learned the truth and were plotting against me. I kept on reading. Bit by bit my mind put together a picture of Jesus. Suddenly I began to recognize that many parts of the picture were matching themselves with words of my forefathers of long ago ... words I have already related to you.

Jesus had the same heart toward all people. He loved the wicked and the good equally. He forgave people their sins. He helped the suffering. He fed the hungry. He welcomed strangers. He never turned His back on someone who asked Him for something. He had a heart of peace and goodness toward everyone. Then I remembered. This is the kind of life my father had lived. I supposed he was still living it right up to now.

But more than that, when bad men wanted to kill Jesus, He did not threaten, or fight, or balk; He let them do what they wished, keeping His dignity even to His death. The Bible calls Him the Lamb of God; and as the sheep is king of animals, God took Jesus out of the grave, gave Him life again, and put Him over all of earth's kings. Now I began to understand Kimbangu and his strange way of acting. Jesus was the Child of the Great Elder Spirit my ancestors had taught me about. His death had darkened and shaken the earth; His spirit was still walking about among us.

Long ago, when fighting wanted to destroy the founders of our tribe, innocent blood was drained onto the ground, and Tshiyamba gave her life, that sinful acts be forgotten, and that a new covenant of peace be established. Why was the innocent blood of Jesus drained upon the ground? Was it not to make appeasement so that our sinful acts might be forgotten? Why did Jesus give His life? Was it not that we stop fighting, swear ourselves to a new covenant, be reconciled to one another, and live in peace? Katombe had asked the earth to rise up and take vengeance upon the one breaking the covenant; and to destroy him and curse his seed. Without knowing it, I had ridiculed and despised the covenant Jesus had died to make for my peace. If I did not change my ways, what kind of curse would befall me?

Reading pages from the Bible and thinking these thoughts began to change me. On Fridays when I went to the market, my heart no longer craved pleasures my friends had brought me; it craved for a new sheet. What power was there in these words that they began disturbing my lusts? My insides began to tremble for joy.

In our way of thinking, a palm tree gives a person all his needs for life: it gives him nuts to eat, raphia fiber to make his cloth, and fronds to build him a place to sleep. Its wealth does not all appear in a day. The seed does not sprout a trunk; it sprouts a tiny soft pointed leaf. In sufficient time, the other things follow.

I knew that the words of this new affair were sprouting. If I persevered in reading them, would not all their treasure follow? Their power to change me showed that they were true. God really loved me. He would accept me. It remained for me to find how to give myself to Him.

One day a guard came and said, "The prison director is calling for you."

Fear caught me. I had been in prison for six years. Had someone told on me? These good affairs which I was beginning to discover, were they all to be for nothing? My fingers felt along the edges of my belt. I was taken to the office, and stood before the Belgian director.

"Maweja, how are your affairs these days?"

"I have no problem."

"We are interested in you. For many months we have been watching you. We have asked guards to bring reports. Their reports have been good. We would like to give you the authority of watching over others; this will show us if anger still rules you, or if you have learned to master it. The prison foreman has finished his sentence. He showed the maturity and strength of a wise man. He has been released. We would like for you to replace him."

Guilt Brings Deliverance **14**

My new work made me a mediator between prisoners and prison authorities. I watched over those calling prison roll every morning; I took their reports to the director. During meals, I was to pass among the tables to make sure everyone ate quietly. During daytime I was to talk with prisoners to understand their feelings; if I found a group of them grumbling and discontented and wanting to defy authority, I was to report it to the director.

This new responsibility made me weigh the value of the kind of life I was living. Could I wear two faces forever? When in the copper mine, the rules of those over us made us wear two faces, and I said I couldn't live with it. Was it right that I now be content with it? Truly, my custom of reading the Bible sheets was reducing my desire for evil; but a cooking pot long neglected does not clean easily. I now felt in my heart that God was willing to forgive me; but would He keep wanting to forgive me while I kept doing evil? Would He wait until all my sins fell off one by one like leaves from a dying tree, and then still forgive me?

I was a person with mistakes; but I was not unintelligent. With my good sense, I had chosen to follow this path. What had I hoped to find in it? I had to break the lid off the box they had locked me in. I had to see that I was growing; that I was progressing; that I was becoming a person in my own right. By this means I would become a person of dignity, a person of worth, as the Creator wants each of us to be. By this means, I would expose the falsehood of ideas other people held about us; I would lift from my tribe and from my race the humiliation which burdened them; they would be respected as people of value equal to that of all people everywhere.

Since choosing that path, many years had passed. What had I found?

In a way I did not understand, demons of evil had taken possession of me; they had made me such a champion of wickedness that what self-respect I once had was wiped out; and I was now left only with shame.

How could I bring respect to my tribe when I flouted its teachings? As the wind bends the stem of a flower and turns its face away from the sun; so these powers had turned my back on all the teachings of my forefathers. They taught me to respect my superiors; now, unless respecting them would help me, I held them in contempt. They taught me to be kindhearted to those in need; it now pleased my heart to be cruel to them. My tribal fathers once taught me that a man and woman lying together was a sacred matter for husband and wife; I scorned such thinking. They were known as people of peace; people knew me for my violence. They believed that the spirits of their dead took vengeance on those who transgressed their laws; I had no such fear.

These thoughts began to crush me with sorrow. By my way of living, I was defying all that my forebears had taught me; I had forsaken the journey bag they had woven for me. I knew my relatives outside prison had carried news of me to my father. I had broken all my vows to him; I had destroyed his hopes for me. I had brought my family and tribe and race no honor; only shame. As I now was, they would disown me.

In the tribal system, everybody cared for everybody; each person had whatever he needed. Here nobody cared for anybody; I had nothing. It was just as I had learned when a child: I was disloyal to my tribe; and so I was destroying myself. These were the things I had found in pursuing this path; and I could not yet see its end.

But had I not begun to see glimmers of light in my darkness? Because of reading the Bible sheets, I was now coming to believe that God wanted to forgive me. The prison director showed faith in me; he wanted to count me as a person of value. Were these affairs not good? Were they not as hands reaching out to help me? Was there a single happy good thing I could hope to get from continuing in this path which had brought me only sadness and evil?

Then, one after another, I began to recall pieces of wisdom from my childhood. They rebuked me for my foolishness.

"The antelope died on the prairie because it forgot where the forest was."

"Greedy crow, if you keep scratching in the garbage pit, one day you'll not know a worm from a scorpion."

"It is your own tool that is slitting your throat."

"Leopard, stop your rapaciousness; it is good conduct which will win you esteem."

"Will you not stop chasing the forest parrot even when it flees to the marshes to hide? You're a murderer. Now in prison, you still torment and terrorize people. How will you ever be saved?"

"You'll not wake up until you die; you'll not begin to listen until you hear the munching of maggots."

These words of my fathers, coming from the happiness of my childhood, heaped upon me guilt. Night came. My guilt allowed me no rest. I lay on my platform in the darkness. Those around me were making the sounds of heavy sleep. My badness hung itself upon a curtain, and began to pass before my eyes. I could not carry this burden. I sought deliverance from it. I wanted to die.

While my mind was suffering thus, a light began to appear above me. I fastened my eyes upon it. This light was so pure that all other light I had ever seen seemed dirty. It grew until its brightness wanted to burn into every corner of me. Then I recalled that shining face which had appeared to me three times when I was lying on the floor of my cell years ago. Affair of wonder that outreaches the mind to believe . . . that Person was

87

still pursuing me! When I understood who it was, that moment the words came to me:

" . . . why are you tormenting me? I am Jesus . . ."

Then before my eyes began to pass slowly, one by one, every person I had ever tormented . . . every white person . . . every soldier . . . every woman . . . every prisoner. In passing, each one looked at me. In their faces I saw their pain. It was plain to me now. I had tormented each one as just a human body; but I had been tormenting Jesus. The light kept burning me; and with it, I burned in shame. I could not keep watching these people. I closed my eyes to shut them out. My heart melted into hot oil. My bitterness was washed from me. My pride burned up like a blade of dry grass. My strength was broken. All desire to fight was finished. I wept and wept, like a lost child being found. Finally, that light shined upon me a love and pity for those around me. Then it slowly went away.

What was this affair which had overcome me? Who could explain it to me? How was I to answer to it? That Jesus was really accepting me surpassed my mind to understand. I ate nothing for three days.

I could not rid myself of guilt for the evil things I had done; but one thing gave me great joy: I wanted to only love those around me. How could I show them that my heart had been turned around, and that now I really loved them? They would not believe me. "Another one of his deceitful plots to hurt us," they would say.

Finally, I thought of a plan. I would turn things around. They were accustomed to suffering for the sake of my happiness. Now I would suffer for their happiness. I would serve them.

True, I was their foreman; but I must do things which would show them that I counted myself to be the lowest person among them. By being their servant, perhaps with the passing of days I could recompense them for all the evil I had done them; then Jesus might have mercy on me, and lift my burden of guilt.

You may find it hard to understand the things this way of thinking compelled me to do. If this is true, perhaps it is because you have never felt in your body and mind the burden of such wickedness as mine.

I refused to eat good food with all the other prisoners. When they were done, I ate the remaining scraps. From time to time when a guard came into the sleeping room at night to ask who was making noise, I would take responsibility for it so that I would be whipped in the place of others.

At the end of our sleeping room was a large half-drum which men used as a toilet during the night; I put my second pair of short trousers beside it for men to use as a wiping cloth; every morning I asked men to put the drum on my head; I carried it to the toilet pit along the far wall and dumped it. I washed and dried my trousers for them to use again.

I asked the white man director to unlock the cell of prisoners whose minds were broken. When he hesitated, I asked him, "Don't you want me to do my work of looking after other prisoners?" Their clothing was tattered; their hair was full of lice; their bodies stank. I took them to the water pit along the right-hand wall; I soaped and bathed their bodies, and put fresh clothes upon them. Then I sat with them in their cell, put my arm around them and comforted them. I thanked Jesus that I could serve Him in these ways.

No one understood. The director would look at me, shake his head and say, "Maweja, Maweja, what has happened to you?" Prisoners said, "The one who was a lion is now carrying our excrement. Has he gone completely crazy?"

With the passing of days my load of guilt began to lighten. I continued reading my sheets from the Bible. One day I read a verse which said that the blood of Jesus Christ washes us from all sin.[7] So that is why Jesus promised us that if we come to Him, He will take our burden and give us rest.[8] From that day on I trusted in the power of Jesus' blood to cleanse me; I hoped it would overpower my demons; I left the burden of all my sins with Him; and I received rest in my heart which has stayed with me clear up to this moment when I write you these words.

I Recall Pieces of Wisdom **15**

There was no doubt about it; a new heart was creating itself within me. As my mind began to lay hold on this truth, I began to think more about my father. With the passing of these years, he could not fail to have heard of my manner of living. He knew that I had renounced the things he had taught me; I had broken all my vows to him; I had killed a person in anger; I was in prison. That thought now brought much suffering to my heart.

I had no hope of ever being released; I could never fulfill the hopes my father had for me. But if somehow news could now reach him that I had changed my life; that I was again walking in the ways he had taught me; then his heart would know some comfort.

There was one thing I could do to strengthen my feet in walking this new path; that was to fill my mind with wisdom from the Bible. If reading these few sheets helped me this much, what help might I find if I read all of them? Kayembe, the first person to give me a page, and another prisoner named Samalenge also wanted to learn more about Jesus. As I was over them now, they kept begging me to arrange a way for them to receive the Words of God. Soldier guards saw how my heart had been turned around. Now some of them were my good friends. One day I spoke to one of them.

"When you go outside tonight, I want you to get me a Book

of God, and a box of candles."

"If I am caught bringing such things into prison, I will be punished."

"Stop being afraid. I'm foreman of the prison. You have already seen with your eyes how I have taken punishment for others. I'll suffer in your place. Here is money. Keep what remains for yourself."

He brought candles and a Bible. Kayembe, Samalenge and I met in secret. We tore off the Bible's cover and discarded it in the toilet pit. Then we tore the book into three parts: Kayembe took the books of Genesis through Second Samuel; Samalenge took the books from First Kings through Malachi; and I took the part of Matthew through Revelation. We swore ourselves to a covenant that if they caught one of us with his part, he would accept whatever punishment came, even death, rather than expose the others.

That night when lights were turned out, I tucked the edges of my blanket into the sides of the platform above me to make it a curtain enclosing me. I tucked it around beneath me. Then I lit a candle and read. Every night I read. I finished my part and exchanged it for another.

My heart drove me to eat up the Book of God like a wind-driven fire eats up dry prairie grass. I chewed what I ate until no taste was left; then swallowed it. I studied this way night after night for three years. Words of the Bible did not strike me hard at once, like a rainstorm. They fell upon me slowly and quietly, for a long time, like the wetness of a heavy fog. This book led me to great treasure which still causes me to marvel, and which I have never exhausted.

What I read took me back to my childhood. Pieces of knowledge from the Bible caught fire like torches and began lighting up the cave of my darkness. So many of the customs of Jesus' tribe and of my tribe were the same that I came to believe that, surely, the Bible must have been written by my ancestors. I had tied myself to Jesus by my faith in Him; now on top of this, I came to feel that truly I was linked to the people of Jesus in my flesh and blood. I was once believing that my tribe and race were matters of shame; and that their customs were to be scorned.

Look at my foolishness. How wrong I had been. Matter of joyous surprise reaching from earth to heaven, these things were sources of great wealth! How can I explain this to you? I will try to gather this harvest of thoughts into three different bundles: affairs of a tribe, affairs within the family, and affairs of the Great Elder Spirit.

Affairs of a Tribe

The forefathers of Jesus were of the tribe of Israel. Like my people in the days of grandfather, the people of Israel lived as a tribe separate from others; their kingdom was made up of villages; sometimes a village was begun by a family.[9] There was much fighting between the people of Israel and people of other tribes living near them. They could not go on long journeys to trade with others. Only by great cunning and great strength, they stayed alive.

The tribe of Israel was ruled by a chief. He was chosen by members of the tribe. He was anointed with oil, as our people had anointed Chief Katombe.[10] When a chief died, he was replaced by his firstborn son.[11]

As it was with my ancestors, circumcision was a mark which kept the forefathers of Jesus different from people surrounding them; they refused to give a daughter to one uncircumcised; they refused to eat with him; they called such an one "unclean."[12] This custom guarded the purity of the tribe. A man married more than one wife, and thus replenished the numbers of people in his tribe.

I pondered our understanding of spilling blood upon the ground beneath us. The wisdom of my forefathers and that of the people of Israel was the same. The earth was like a living person who mourns when innocent blood is spilt upon it; such blood pollutes it.[13]

My tribal fathers believed that the spirits of their dead remained to live in the ground; if they had died wrongly, their blood cried out from the ground for vengeance. If the anger of earth was not appeased, it would rise up and destroy the guilty one and would curse his seed. Only the blood of an innocent sacrifice could quiet it.

After Cain killed Abel, God said to him, "The voice of your brother's blood is crying to me from out of the earth." A curse was declared upon him.[14] A chief of Israel named Ahab killed Naboth to steal his field. The ground of that field took vengeance. Having soaked up the blood of Naboth, it then soaked up the blood of Chief Ahab and his seed.[15] A man named Zophar said the wicked will never find a path of escape, because "heaven will reveal his iniquity, and earth will rise up against him."[16] How did the people of Israel escape the anger of the slaying angel? By draining upon their thresholds the blood of a lamb.[17]

Like my ancestors, they felt great responsibility to settle crimes justly. When the evildoer was exposed, they recompensed eye for eye, tooth for tooth, wound for wound.[18] When a wife was accused of adultery, the priest would prepare a medicine cup to establish the truth.[19] Among the people of Tshiyamba and the people of Israel, one guilty of adultery was often slain; one fornicating with a virgin girl was forced to marry her, or to recompense her parents the part of the bride price lost when he ruined her virginity.[20] When a child rebelled against the authority of his father, our laws were the same: "Everyone who curses his father or mother shall surely be put to death."[21] If our tribal judges failed to complete justice upon an evil doer, God would complete it by bringing calamity upon him.[22]

Affairs Within the Family

The important affairs in any family are three: marriage, birth and death.

Marriage:

In some tribes, a young man uses girls like a perching bird uses the branches of trees. My tribe was different. The fathers say, "Pay bride price for a girl, and you will always have someone to grind your meal." In the Bible Jacob worked for his in-laws seven years to pay bride price for his wife Rachel.[23]

Abraham sent ten camel-loads of wealth to his relatives that they give their daughter Rebekah into marriage with his son Isaac.[24] Hosea paid silver and grain that his bride be faithful to him.[25]

The law of Israel said, "If a husband dies without a child, let not his wife be married to an outsider; her husband's brother will take her to wife . . ."[26] The law of Tshiyamba was the same. Long ago a man did not thus perform his duty, and the widow gave herself to harlotry.[27] This is a problem that troubles our people up to today. Sarah, the first wife of Abraham, was ruler of the compound, no one disputing her authority.[28]

Childbirth: My fathers believed that a woman's main work upon earth is to bear children. Didn't the Creator say it was thus?[29] It is the custom of our women to bless one another with words like those with which they blessed Rebekah when she entered marriage: "Be thou the mother of thousands . . . and may your offspring inherit the land of your enemies."[30] Children which a woman bears are her reward from God; they are an inheritance given us from the All Powerful One;[31] the firstborn male inherits twice the things of those who are born after him.[32]

Even the private affairs of our women and of the women of Israel harmonize. When the women of Tshiyamba come from the period of menstrual uncleanness, they offer their husbands white meat for their purification; the women of Israel offered the priest two pigeons.[33] To allure their husbands, our women use tshipambu medicine; the women of Israel used mandrakes.[34] As was the affair with Israel, offending for barrenness and joy for childbirth are inside us like the air we breathe.[35]

I have already related the strong punishment for adultery and fornication. On top of this, no child is to see the nakedness of a parent or close relative; to do so may lock up the child's own birth powers. Children are not to play with one another's nakedness; those guilty of such sin could bring a curse upon the tribe. When I read the laws of the tribe of Israel which refuse the viewing of nakedness within a family, my mind showed me

94

a picture of the elders of Tshiyamba sitting in council and answering with one heart, "Let it be thus forever."[36]

A woman bearing a child had to live alone until she fulfilled her days of purification. It was the same in the tribe of Israel.[37] Babies were given names with special meanings. This custom began with the Creator Himself. He named Abram "Abraham" meaning "the father of many nations."[38] He named Jacob "Israel" meaning "he who strived with God."[39] The people of Israel continued the custom.[40] When the Son of the Great Elder Spirit appeared upon the earth, the angel ordered Mary to name him "Jesus" meaning "savior", because His work was to save people from their sins.[41]

Our people composed songs, and sang them on births and other important occasions. After God delivered the people of Israel from slavery, they prepared a song, and while singing it, danced for joy.[42] Moses prepared for them a song to help them remember the affairs of their fathers.[43] When they defeated their enemies in war, they sang.[44] When Hannah bore her first child, she prepared her own song and sang.[45]

Death:

When a tribemate dies, we have great mourning. We wail and sing dirge songs in memory of him. We honor the graves of our dead; we believe their spirits remain there to watch us and to guide our affairs. In this too, we are one with the tribe of Israel. They mourned for Joseph[46]; for Moses[47]; for the daughter of Jairus.[48] Nehemiah gave great honor to the graves of his fathers.[49]

Affairs of the Great Elder Spirit

Our fathers had many beautiful names with which to describe the Creator; and all of them harmonize with what the Book reveals Him to be. He is the only One who has been alive forever. He is the Knower of all affairs. His pureness is brighter than the sun. The only thing that has power to clean a man from his sins before the Creator is the drained blood of a living creature offered in sacrifice.[50] To cleanse a cursed house, our tribal diviner used two white chickens; the priest of Israel used two birds.[51] While our diviner believed a chicken had power to carry sins away into the high grass, the priest of Israel put the same faith in a goat.[52]

God showed us things through dreams. He did the same to Abraham, Jacob, Joseph, Daniel and others. Israel gave the firstfruits of their harvests to God, and were careful not to neglect widows and orphans.[53]

The Bible now taught me more adequately great events tribal fathers had related to us: how the first man and woman sinned; how men built a tower to reach the sky; and how darkness covered the earth the day that the Son of the Great Elder Spirit was killed.

You who read these words, perhaps I have wearied you; perhaps the customs of your ancestors likewise fit those of the ancestors of Jesus, and so in all that I have said, there is nothing remarkable. But I was as a man born blind who now began to see.

Every custom of my people which I found in the tribe of Israel told me that I was a person of value. Outsiders had not first brought to us the affair of God; it appeared to have come straight to us from the far north, carried on the lips of generations of my tribal ancestors. I saw that my journey bag which I'd thought could be scorned, was a thing of value which surpassed me to measure. My tribe and my heritage were not my shame; they were my treasure.

I also came to see how far my manner of living had led me astray from what my Creator wanted, what my tribe taught me, and what my heart had been craving. My tribe had laws which curbed pride and lust and anger. These laws had not been established for nothing. Even my ancestors recognized that evil, if it were not restrained, would destroy their life of community; any person living in such a manner had to be removed from among them.

Everyone must be proud of his value as a person. He needs to have dignity; he needs to understand his self-worth. It is not wrong to desire these things; it is not wrong to seek them. But when pride made me want to be the master of others, then all kinds of evil followed. These evils enslaved me, and destroyed the self-worth I longed for. Now it seemed that the lesson I was being taught by my forefathers, and the Bible, and the example of Kimbangu was one:

Evils which war within us, if not controlled, destroy our self-worth. Mastering these evils will bring back to us our self-worth. And the measure that I was able to tame these evils which wanted to rule me, to that measure I would find self-worth. This was the affair I now wanted to wrestle with: how to tame my sins, and thereby truly come to be master of myself.

As foreman, I no longer went to the meat market. If people wanted to see me, they had to come hunt me at prison. One day three of my friends came looking for me.

"Bad news from your home village has reached us."

"What kind of news?"

"Your father has died."

"How did you find out?"

"Travelers; they were at your village when the people were in mourning."

"Why did he die?"

They looked at one another. One of them shrugged.

"As God willed it."

"Was he sick?"

"They said he had been troubled with sickness for a long time."

My father had always been strong and healthy. I could not understand this.

"What kind of sickness was it?"

"Well, they said it was sickness of sorrow."

"Sorrow about what?"

One sighed and spoke.

"They said it started when he learned you were put into prison. Then when he heard you would be in prison for all of your life, his sorrow surpassed him in strength. He could not accept it. He fasted. He made offerings to the spirits. He paid witch doctors to make strong medicines that would liberate you; he followed all their rituals and abstinences. When all these things failed, sorrow overwhelmed him and, finally he died."

My insides became empty with sadness. News that my life had been turned around never reached him. My broken vows had saddened him. And now, my evil way of living had killed him. Just as the forefathers say: "It's the child you love too much who will break your only gourd of drinking water."

"Oh my Lord," I prayed, "something very good happened; you showed me that I am a person of great worth. Now something very bad has happened; my evil conduct has brought my father to his death. If I am a person of such great value in Your eyes, how can You want me to stay locked inside this prison for all of my remaining days? Will you never allow me to do any other kind of work for You forever? Is there no way for me ever to repay my people and to repay my father for what I have done?"

Meetings in the Shadow of Death 16

About the same time I lost my father, during my seventh year in prison, we watched another person die of sorrow. The burden of Kimbangu to be released began to overwhelm him. All day long, day after day, he would walk from one prison wall to the other, and back again. Then he began fasting. When numerous plates of food accumulated, they would punish him. He would not change his mind. They locked him into his cell. His body began to waste away.

Once in awhile, when a prisoner died in the cell of torment, guards would carry the corpse past the cell of Kimbangu. At this time Kimbangu would stand, begin to breathe heavily, and tremble over his whole body, as if in a trance.

"I feel great power wants to break out through me, but there is nothing I can do about it," he would say when we asked him why he acted this way. "If they carry my corpse from this place, I'll rise up from the dead to do the work of God." Bit by bit, his body weakened. Then he began passing most of his time lying quietly on his cement platform, as though ill.

One morning when we were getting up, word came that during the night Kimbangu had died. Soldier guards and a few prisoners took him outside and buried him. Because he had said he would rise from the dead, soldiers guarded his grave day and night. Finally, when they came back to prison, they said, "Kimbangu was mistaken; we watched his grave a whole week; nothing happened."

The death of Kimbangu shook my insides. His sentence and mine were the same. Is this the way my life would end? I had never known a man who walked with God like Kimbangu had. If he, good as he was, died in prison, how could I ever be released? I had counted him to be an extremely valuable person. By his kindness to those who persecuted him; by his sharing his bit of meat with everybody; he was the first to show me that I must love my neighbor as myself. What other person was left to show us by his words and deeds, the love and goodness of God? His teaching had strengthened all of us. Without him, the poison in men's hearts would be left to grow unhindered; and I as foreman, could expect trouble.

One day I was in the storehouse, looking for some things which were lost. I came upon an old Bible. It was Kimbangu's. On many many of its pages, lines were drawn under words; and notes were written alongside them. I also found others books of his: a New Testament; a small book of Romans; and a notebook full of sermons and study thoughts written in his handwriting. During his early years in prison, they had let him use these things. Then a new director came; he took the books away from him, and locked him in his cell. Kimbangu never saw his books again. I took them into the director's office.

"I found these things in the storehouse."

The director took the books, looked through them a bit, and said, "Gather all those things together and burn them."

I obeyed. The director did not know it; but there was another Bible in prison which was not being burned. Its teaching would not die. I did not feel sufficient to walk in the footsteps of Kimbangu. But God was already doing amazing things in my life; I had a great debt to Him. I saw what the teaching of His word did for the prisoners. As their foreman, I was indebted to them. It was up to me to see that, though Kimbangu was dead, the teaching of God's Word among them was not ending. If I never had the opportunity to work for God as a free man, I should not waste the opportunity to work for Him while in prison. The time had come for me to clean up my life of all its

100

sins, and to declare openly to the prisoners what I believed. It already had been decreed anyhow that I was to die here; what did it matter if I died sooner because I was working for God and helping my neighbors?

Because of my hunger to know the Bible and to see it do its work in my life, my heart was open before God. He had been able to drive out of me the demons of anger, liquor and harlotry. But I was still a bond-slave to tobacco.

Upon getting up in the morning, it was my custom to light one cigarette and to not stop until I had smoked ten. When awaking in the middle of the night, my hand had learned to reach out and hunt for my tobacco without my mind telling it to. I now saw that continuing this habit made me like the parrot who talks like something he isn't. I did not need this habit any more. The time had come for me to affirm my liberation from its slavery.

One evening the prisoners were eating. I moved among the cement tables and quietly told them that when they had finished eating, I wanted to meet them in my sleeping room. I went and waited for them. Slowly the room filled, all their faces showing question marks. A few soldier guards had come to watch me. I spoke.

"Comrades, a loin cloth cannot fail to come to know its loins. We live here together; we cannot fail to know each other. You remember me as I was. You see me now. You wonder what has happened to me. I have come to know the Son of Mvidi Mukulu. He is the One who has turned my life around. He is my Lord. To prove His power, I swear before you that I am quitting smoking, liquor, and harlotry as of this day.

"I am not alone in knowing the Son of Mvidi Mukulu; others among you have known Him too. The prison director sees our quietness and thinks that all is soft as a cat's paw. He doesn't know that among us are hidden the claws of deceit and treachery. Why do we keep pursuing such a path? What good thing do we hope to find at its end? Who keeps telling you that it is good to snuff out your light with wickedness, or to keep hiding it under a box?

"Why don't we clean up affairs among us? I beg all of you

who have Mvidi Mukulu in your hearts to declare it from your mouths and to stand with me. Let's begin together. I am foreman of the prison. No one is going to suffer more than I. If it means dying, let's die together. I am forcing no one. You have mouths with which to talk, and I have ears to listen. Do what you think is right."

The men left slowly. They didn't move their tongues . . . only their feet. Three men remained near me; my two friends who were secretly reading their parts of the Bible, and a new person.

"We too know this affair," they said. "As you say, we should stick to it. If it means death, let's all die."

"If your words are true," I replied, "meet me here after supper tomorrow evening. On a piece of scrap paper, write a verse from the Bible, or a song you remember; bring your papers, and we'll teach one another."

Thus we began meeting every day. We began with great courage, not knowing what might happen. We memorized songs and dug treasure from our verses to the limit of our wisdom. This was something strange and new. It had never happened in this prison before.

As time passed, many others were attracted. Some were curious; they came as dogs to sniff the air. Others by one and two, took the vow of death upon themselves and joined us with all their hearts. After a time, those who loved singing formed a choir. We would choose one person to stand and teach.

When meeting in the evenings, we trusted that other prison noises would cover the sound of our singing. When we met at night, we prayed that God would put those over us into strong sleep so they would not come and find us. Soldier guards knew what we were doing; but because I'd been with them a long time, they ignored me. They were saying, "If that condemned man finds a bit of pleasure this way, what does it matter?" Thus we met day after day, no one coming to trouble us.

The prison director did not understand why, but he saw that his prisoners were more content. Fighting was less; shouting in anger was less; whipping with the mfimbu was less. Instead of tying their hearts to do one another evil, men began to see themselves together as sharers of the same suffering. These things made the director happy. He commended me for my work.

One day three men came to see me. They hunted hard for words to speak, as a pregnant woman in pain, who cannot give birth.

"You keep saying that we should clean things up between one another."

"Yes."

One was looking at his bare feet; another was fidgeting with his belt; the lips of the third were hunting for words.

"Didn't the forefathers say, 'Tie your sicknesses to your heart and they will kill you'? Our hearts have carried a sickness for many days. We must get rid of it before it kills us."

"There is still time," I said to help them. "When your spirit enters the realm of the ghosts, there is no calling for a mediator. What sickness?"

"You do not know it. Once we offended you terribly. But now we see that it is foolish for goats to offend one another when they all have buck teeth. We have come to make things right."

"Well . . . in what way was it that you offended me?"

"It happened long ago at Kolwezi, at the time they first caught you."

"Yes."

"You killed a soldier that day."

"Yes."

"Then they brought you into prison; they bound you into a bundle and put you into the torment cell."

"We did wickedly that day," another said. "We were animals. Why did we want to increase your torment?" He shook his head in wonderment.

"What did you do?"

"You remember the anger of the soldiers and of the women. They gathered together their wisdom. They knew you were thirsty. They arranged something for you to drink."

Another picked up his words. "There is only one reason why we accepted to give it to you. We hoped that in helping torment you, the soldier guards might be more merciful to us."

"What was it that you gave me to drink?"

My words turned their faces to the ground.

"Do not fear to tell me. Jesus has taken from me my fangs of vengeance. Old affairs are past."

After a pause, one of them breathed deeply and said, "Women had washed their menstrual cloths in a bucket; that is what they put into the cup."

Almost seven years had passed since then. I marvelled. Why had God protected my life through all these things, and brought me all the way to this day? In spite of all my wickedness, He had forgiven me. He had given back to me the pride and joy of being a person of value. Now the love He had given me for others was making them straighten out matters in their lives. I was still a young man. Did God have nothing else on earth for me to do but to stay here forever? Did He not have power to open these prison doors and liberate me?

I began to pray hard that God would set me free. I came to loathe my imprisonment. At a meeting one night I announced to the Christians, "I am fed up with my bondage. Tomorrow I am fasting. I want to ask God the question, 'Are you going to liberate me or not?' I want His answer."

Some said, "Let God do as He wills; if He wants to do such an amazing thing for you, what can we say?"

Others said, "Remember Kimbangu? God never left him out. Is Maweja more worthy than he? Such a thing won't ever happen."

The next day I ate nothing. Night came. I went to bed. Sleep fled from me. At one o'clock in the morning I arranged my blanket curtain. I took inside with me three candles and my part of the Bible. I began reading. I kept searching for God's answer with weeping until all three candles were finished. Only these words seemed to catch my mind: "As an antelope pants hunting a stream of water, so my heart pants to see God. My heart is thirsty . . . thirsty for the living God. When will I appear before God? Tears have become my food day and night. I will ask God my Rock, 'Have you abandoned me?'" (Psalm 42:1-3).

I stopped and stood my mind on that verse, asking this question times without counting: "My God, my God, have you really abandoned me?" I cried over these words until morning.

God Keeps His Word 17

"The director wants to see you," a prison soldier-guard said.

"What is the matter?"

"They caught a youth reading from part of a book. He says it belongs to you."

I turned and slowly walked ahead of the guard toward the director's office. I had loaned this young man my part of the Bible; I had wanted to help him. He was new in prison, sentenced for stealing.

When my mind thought about covering up the whole affair with a lie, I heard a voice in my heart: "Whoever denies me before the eyes of men, for my part, I will deny him before my Father in heaven." I arrived in front of the director's desk and stood straight, waiting.

"Do you know this young man?"

"Yes."

"Is this your book?"

"Yes."

"How did you get it?"

I was silent.

He looked at his two secretaries.

"Did you give Maweja this book?"

The secretaries knew that I was as a dead person with no hope of ever being released; they didn't want to increase my suffering.

"It must have accidently slipped into the prison mixed up with all the papers and magazines that go in and out of here."

He looked at me.

"Maweja, this matter saddens me greatly. We had thought you might someday get out of your chains. If we ever catch you with a book like this again, you'll never be released; you'll waste away in here forever."

They kept the book and burned it.

I had heard the words from the director's mouth. "We had thought you might someday get out of your chains," he had said. These words stuck in my mind, and wiped out everything else he said. I went to my friend and borrowed another part of the Bible. That night I found words that made my heart leap for joy: "Let his place be empty; let no one else take it" (Acts 1:20).

Then I remembered what God did for the people of Israel in Egypt. It was God who hardened Pharaoh's heart; and it was God who softened it. But before all of this, God had already decided that when the time was sufficient, He would deliver them from their slavery.

The big thing was not that I'd been caught with the Bible. The big thing was that the director had revealed to me the hope that I might someday be set free. This was God's sign to me. I now had the feeling in my heart that when the time was sufficient, God would soften the director's heart, and I would be delivered.

When morning came I gathered the prisoners and told them, "God has answered me. I'll get out of these chains in the few days that are ahead."

Three months passed. I was beginning my ninth year in prison. I became discouraged. I began to feel again that God had deserted me. Every day sorrow grated my stomach like gravel. I covenanted with God, "If the time comes when You have pity on me and break of these chains, whatever appears before me in all of my days ahead that You want to take, it is Yours."

It appears that the heart of that director could not be changed. God removed him and brought us a new one. Every two years each prisoner's report was sent to a court to be studied. When the new director sent in my report, I heard them saying that he had spoken well of me. Some weeks passed.

It was the second month of my ninth year. One night, just after we had been locked inside our sleeping room, we heard the voice of one calling at the door.

"Maweja."

It was the voice of the director.

"Present!"

"Arrange your affairs. Tomorrow you leave."

Ayiiiiiiiiiiiii, what joy! Guards opened the cell doors. Prisoners packed themselves around me. They fought to throw their arms around me and to shake my hand. We rejoiced. We prayed. We sang songs. Then some of them began to worry.

"Your going is our sorrow. Who will replace you as our foreman? If his heart is not like yours, we'll begin suffering again."

"You see what this new director did to help me. His heart is good. You will not suffer as you once did, so long as he is here. I'm asking Samalenge to take my place as leader of the Christians; he was one of those who divided the Bible with me when reading it had the penalty of flogging or the torture cell."

"What are you going to do when you get outside?"

"I am going to the town of Luebo, where they print the *News of the Kasai Peoples* magazine; I hear they have a school to help you learn the Bible. I'm going to study that book until I'm ripe in it; then I'm going to work for God for all the remaining days of my life."

We kept on rejoicing. Morning caught us. I got my travel papers. I thanked the director and told him he'd never see me again.

On that day, the 13th of August, 1953, I walked out of the prison door. I went straight to the church of the Methodist Mission on the main street of Lubumbashi. There on my knees I worshipped and thanked and praised my God.

"Here I am. I'm keeping my covenant. Put me into your work," I told Him.

I got onto the train to begin my journey. I was going to Likasi, where they had first judged me and sentenced me to

107

prison for life. I wanted to pick up a metal chest of my clothing and other things which I'd left with relatives when I was first imprisoned there. Only when the train began to move did my mind begin to comprehend what was happening. It was really removing me from this place. There was no guard with a gun watching me. I was truly a person with freedom. I began to feel like a bird, free and high, fluttering its wings with happiness, with only the open sky around it.

While journeying, my mind began to recall all that had happened to me. Hard affairs had broken my life into pieces. Could I put them together again? What were the lessons all these things could teach me? Pictures passing the windows reminded me of my childhood, and led my mind to a fable I had heard long ago.

Once there was a young crocodile. He detested the way of living of his clan. Every day there was the same manner of acting: they caught and ate fish until there were full; then they laid on the sandbank in the sun until they were hungry. He came to loathe it. He married a wife. Even this did not give him joy. Finally, he vowed in his heart that he must wander in the world and find something better. He left his home on the river sandbank to search for real wealth and happiness.

One day in the forest he met the lion. "I am king of the river," he said to himself, "and he is king of the jungle. If I am clever enough to steal from him his wisdom, I'll steal from him his kingdom also, and will rule everything."

The crocodile made friends with the lion. He learned that the secret of the lion's authority was his great strength. He watched the lion hide behind a high boulder, pounce upon an antelope, kill it, and roar to the shaking of the tree leaves. His heart trembled with excitement. He would learn to do this himself.

After some days the crocodile returned to the boulder and waited. When an antelope came, he leaped with all his strength. But because of his short legs, he dropped helplessly into the path. The antelope hooked him with its horns; it poked his eye; it turned him upside down and trampled on his soft stomach. Then it fled.

The crocodile crawled into the deep forest, His stomach

hurt. His eye swelled shut. He was terribly humiliated. He decided that friendship with the lion was not good; he would search elsewhere for wealth and happiness. After some days, the strength of his hunger exceeded the strength of his shame, and he began his journey again.

One day his good eye showed him what looked like a great black vine slowly crawling up a tree. It was a boa constrictor. He looked at its long tail and slender nose. "It is clear to me now that the lion and I are no relation," the crocodile told himself. "But look at this big snake. Surely it and I are sons of the same ancestor." The snake wound his body around a low limb and waited. After a time, a squirrel came playing among the branches. Quick as lightning, the snake caught it and swallowed it. After a time a forest rat ran beneath the limb; the snake quietly stretched himself out, snatched it and ate it.

The crocodile made friends with the boa constrictor. "Help me learn the joy of catching food this way," he said. The snake got a vine, and with it pulled the crocodile up into the tree. The crocodile laid quietly on the limb, watching with his good eye. When time passed, a chipmunk came running along its path. The crocodile tried to stick out his head quick as lightning; he fell off the limb and hit the ground. One leg hit a rock; it was pulled from its socket. Slowly he dragged himself off into the jungle, saying nothing.

Days passed. Mr. Crocodile was no longer yearning for happiness and wealth. His body was maimed and weak. He just wanted something to eat. One day he saw a baboon sitting in a tree.

"Please, sir," he said, "could you help me find something to eat?"

"Do you eat land turtles?" the baboon replied. "Follow this path, and you will leave the forest and enter tall prairie grass. There, if you hunt well, you will see the great round backs of prairie turtles. They move slowly; with your sick body, you should be able to catch them."

The crocodile left the forest and entered the grass. Soon his eye showed him the black forms of turtles under their shells. A huge one was close to him. It was not moving. The crocodile slowly crawled close to it, opened his jaws wide, and bit it with all his strength. His teeth broke. His jaw hurt. His mouth was full of dirt. He had bitten an ant hill.

Mr. Crocodile was sick of traveling. Strangers had deceived him. His body was wasted and maimed. He started back toward his sandbank home. When he got near, he saw an amazing thing. Outside his home was a line of 12 young crocodiles. Each had a pile of different kinds of wealth: goats, pigs, shining cooking pans, bolts of new cloth. Never since he was born had he seen so many good things. Two brothers came out to greet him.

"Where have you been?" they asked. "We've been waiting for you a long time. After you left, the eggs your wife laid in the sand hatched 12 daughters. These young men waiting here have brought their bride-price wealth to marry them."

Like Mr. Crododile, I had wasted myself looking for wealth and happiness elsewhere; but both had been in the things I had once despised. Now I was going back home to find them. I journeyed with a light and happy heart.

But ahead of me was also war; the kind of war that every strong Christian must keep fighting within himself until the body dies.

My First Test: Lust 18

I arrived at Likaski. I found my clan mates. They were very happy to see me. I stayed with them that night. The next morning I prepared my things for the journey. They cooked food for me. I ate it.

"Where are you going now?" they asked.

"I want to go back to Kolwezi, where troubles first caught me. I want to say goodbye to my old friends there; then I will go to Luebo." I doubted if I had sufficient money for the trip; but I did not want to beg.

"To Kolwezi? We have a tribemate here who would like to send a child back to her parents; they live at Kolwezi. Would you take her and see that she arrives at home?"

"That is no problem."

A person went and brought her. She was a girl almost old enough for marriage. Her face had the beauty of youth; her body was matured. I had not been close to a woman for a long time. She attracted me powerfully.

"Fine," I said. "I'll take good care of her."

We boarded the train. I chose a compartment. We would be together the whole day. She sat down on one side. I sat down beside her. We were alone. The train began its journey. We began talking about this and that. Friendship began drawing us together. Then, with the shaking of the train, our bodies began leaning against each other.

After a man has been locked inside of prison for years, when he first gets out, how does his body respond to a woman? Desire began to torment me. After a time, I put my arm around her shoulder. I felt my blood catch on fire. Craving wanted to split me. In times past I had not restrained myself in such matters; it had been my custom to finish the affair. But now it was different. Within me there was war. While in my body lust tortured me, my heart rebuked me. The one said, "Why do you torment yourself insufferably hour after hour for nothing?" The other said, "So soon are you going to allow the devil to push you into a pit?"

I began to pray. "Lord," I said, "You know what has always been the weakness of this my body. On my second day out of prison, why do you let me be caught in a trap like this?"

Then I remembered words from the Bible: "The man who endures temptation will be blessed; for after he has passed the test, he will receive the crown of life which the Lord has promised all who love Him. When a person is tempted, don't let him say, 'God is tempting me'; but he is tempted when he is drawn by is own lust; and when lust conceives, it will bear sin" (James 1:12-15).

I fought war within myself like I had never known since I was born. Finally we arrived at a station where we had to change trains. I got off and walked around outside, praying.

"My God, You brought me out of prison, truly," I said. "But You see all the troubles I'm having. You know I want to go to Kolwezi to show my old friends that I'm still on this earth, and how my life has been turned around. You know also, that if I spend my little money for a ticket to go there, I'll have nothing left for the long trip to Luebo. I don't want to stumble. This kind of fighting weakens me. If You are really fighting this war with me, please show me. Couldn't You put love in the ticket seller's heart so I'll spend no more of my money to get there?" Didn't You say that You are the Way?"

When I went to the window the man said, "Don't buy a ticket now; wait to one side over there." After some time we saw them passing us all through the gate and onto the train. We found a compartment. She sat down. I vowed in my heart, "If Jesus is with me like that to fight this war, I'll not allow my lust to draw me into temptation." I sat down along on the bench facing her. I stayed there until we arrived at Kolwezi.

Remember what I had promised my friends here the last time I was with them? I was not returning to them in the clouds of the sky; I was returning in another manner.

When I arrived at the work camp, a great crowd of people gathered around me. Because of my violence and loose living, I was very well known.

"Maweja our hero has returned!" they cried. "Let's have a welcoming celebration at the cafe tonight!"

That evening the cafe was full of people. I was shown to the table of honor. Bartenders poured drinks for everybody. I refused beer; I asked for orange soda. A few people saw it, had questioning on their faces a moment, than again turned their minds to the celebrating.

Then they began performing skits to remind us of the things we had done together. A large man came through the door. Someone had made for him a wig of long loose hair. He strutted into the center of the people, clacking his shoes loudly. Kneeling in front of a person wearing a long white robe, he tilted back his head, and opened his mouth. The robed person imitated giving him the holy food. People laughed and clapped until the walls shook. Then the big man stood in front of people seated at a table. He lifted a glass of beer and said, "Do you want my strength? This is my blood. Drink it, all of you." People cheered and yelled. My face smiled; but my heart felt only pity and sadness.

Then my old friends gathered around me, and said, "We the apostles who ate your flesh and drank your blood; we are still here."

I looked at them and smiled. "It is me you see with your eyes, truly. But it is not the old Maweja; the old Maweja has disappeared. I have been changed. I have no desire to be your hero. I don't want to be lord of anybody. Another Lord has overpowered me. He has put me into His work instead."

They stared at one another in amazement. "Once this man was proud and ferocious; he craved liquor and licentiousness.

By what manner are words of this "other Lord" business coming out of his mouth? Where did he learn it?"

"God got hold of me and turned my life around while I was in chains," I explained. I shook hands with them all, and said goodbye. This was the second war I had encountered and won.

When I vowed to glue my heart to the words of Jesus and to obey them without wavering, I found power to refuse sin and to speak boldly for Him. My heart rejoiced exceedingly. I entered the train and began the long journey for Luebo.

During the days of that journey, I guarded myself well. I had time to think about what happens to the person who is walking with Jesus. I had not realized it, but in prison I was guarded from many testings. Now that I was free, I discovered the war that the Christian must fight.

At first the fierceness of this inner fighting perplexed me. But when I began to realize that I had renounced my allegiance to an old chief while still living in his country, I began to understand.

In our land, every adult must buy a government identification card. On this card is his picture, his name, his age, the names of his parents, and where he lives. He must carry this card with him at all times. Any civil authority may ask to see it. It proves that a person is a citizen of the country and a member of the country's only political party, of which our president is founder and head. By carrying this card, you are pledging loyalty to the president and obedience to the laws of his party.

The Bible teaches us that this earth is under the authority of the devil. Before Jesus left He prayed to the Father, "Don't take them off the earth; but save them from the Evil One" (John 17:15).

Christians are on the devil's earth, but refuse to buy his identification card. They refuse to obey his laws. So the devil comes and asks them, "You don't want to buy my card? You don't want to follow my rules? You refuse to live under my authority? What are you doing here?" He'll give them no peace. He'll persecute them. He'll wage war to destroy them.

Jesus said, "I tell you these things beforehand so that you

may have peace within yourselves. While you are on the earth, you will suffer. But rejoice; I have overcome the world" (John 16:33). That suffering is not from lack of food or of drink or of clothing. Satan is tormenting me that I buy his card, that I swear allegiance to him and obey him. Then he'll be able to bind me with fornication, pride, foul language, and wrath. While we are on the devil's earth, we cannot be loyal subjects of Jesus unless we are perpetually hard-headed rebels against the devil. I'll relate more about waging this war later.

God had done amazing things for me. He had restored to me an understanding of my worth; He had delivered me from prison. He was teaching me how to tame the sins which once ruled me; and now I hoped He would put me into school so that I could learn how to work for Him.

I arrived at Luebo. I went to the mission station and presented myself to the missionaries. They listened to my story. I took the test to enter Bible School, and passed. Then the missionaries said, "Truly, you know God. You should learn more about the Bible. You should work for Him as an evangelist. However, a man in such work in this land cannot maintain a name of honor unless he is married. Three months remain before class begins. Why don't you return to your home village and look for a wife?"

I Seek a Wife 19

As I thought about arriving at my home village, my mind was in turmoil. How would my people receive me? They all knew that I had renounced my upbringing; I had pursued a manner of living which brought shame to them. There was no way for me to erase it from their memory. The path you wear through high-grass stems won't disappear, even if you burn them, the proverb says; and if a palm nut is guilty, its tree cannot claim innocence.

In spite of all that, it was my hope that my people would reinstate me with honor, and help provide me a wife. My people had sayings which showed the generosity of their hearts: "Don't be ashamed to call for help to put out your fire, even if you started it." They also had sayings which showed that their justice could be severe: "You aren't worthy of eating bean leaves with your fingers; and you're preparing to eat beef?"

Suppose that my tribe accepted to restore me; what woman would accept to live with me?

A rumor had spread: my sentence was that I had to do the prison terms of two people, it said; now the white people had released me and had told me, "Go catch another person; bring that person back to us to do your second term."

Another rumor said, "He was released because he agreed to catch people from among us and take them to the white man to eat."

Also women would say, "He's a murderer; the ghost of that person is on him. Anytime it pleases, it can seize and kill someone in revenge." Moreover, scars were all over my body; as long as a woman lived with me, she would look at them and recall what an evil man I had been.

Yet, what other path was left for me but to look to my tribe for help? A man cannot live without the pot that cooks his beans; and as the axe must bruise itself to split wood, so a man must torment himself for a woman. I must try.

I did not want my arrival to stir up the feelings of the whole tribe. I did not want to embarrass them. I hoped everything would be kept within the family. I would go to the house of my father's eldest brother, Kazadi. I would first reconcile myself with him, and then hope that he and his brothers would hew the path ahead of me. Perhaps this way I could finish my business quietly, and after a few days, leave again.

I walked from the train station to my village and arrived in the heat of the day. My Uncle Kazadi was seated in his yard, and saw me coming. He shouted as he rushed toward me.

"Ayiiiiiii, Elder Spirit of love, look who has arrived! Our child Maweja! Come, everybody!" He threw his arms around me, released me, and looked at me.

"My uncle, I have a matter to talk over with you."

"We also," he replied, his face bright with happiness. "We have lots of matters to talk over with you. How many days have passed since we saw you!"

People were yelling to one another the full length of the village. They were running from everywhere . . . uncles, their wives, cousins whose faces my mind struggled to recall, and children I did not know. They began pushing me, slapping my shoulders, and shaking my hands.

"Maweja, child of Kalala!"

"Look how he has matured!"

"Storm always drives the children home!"

"Listen, my uncle." I said. I don't want to stir up everybody. Let us talk the matter over between the two of us."

"Don't talk like a stupid one! You are our guest. We don't ask a guest what is in his stomach until we have fed him. You

117

were as a dead person. You have returned to us alive. Do you refuse for us to celebrate?"

There was no other way. Animals were slain. Food was gathered. That evening we had a feast. It appeared I was their hero. All the families of our clan were present, and also many important people from other clans of the tribe. Though I was happy my people had accepted me, my heart was not at ease.

What was all this leading me to? What were the matters they were waiting to discuss with me?

I had wanted to find myself a wife and leave. But my people had their way of doing things. Many times I had heard the elders say, "Don't berate a goat for easing itself; its manure may help grow your food." They ate, drank, sang and danced; I watched, smiled and waited.

The next morning my uncles and our clan leaders came and sat in a circle to talk with me.

"You cannot know our joy that we are seeing your face again," Uncle Kazadi began. "We had feared that you would never return. It is true that you at first failed. But you've been to many far-away places. You've learned many things. Now you will be even better able to fulfill our expectations."

"What is it you are hoping for?"

They began speaking slowly at first; then their words tumbled out like a basket spilling ears of corn.

"Ever since your father died, we have found no one to take his place. As you know, he longed for the day when you would do it. We had the same hopes. Now they will be realized."

"During the years of your childhood, we saw how you had inherited the gifts of your father. The tribe wants you to be official greeter and caretaker of the guests, as was your father."

"And on top of that honor, we want you to be chief of our clan."

"We don't know if in your journeyings you found the wealth you desired or not. It makes no matter. You remember how your father with his wives worked hard and accumulated wealth. You are the firstborn; you are the rightful heir."

"You will remember that your father used his wealth in a way that brought strength and honor to the whole tribe. Now that you have arrived among us, it is our hope that you will marry wives, build your compound, and progress in the path your father began."

"Wealth for bride prices is no problem. There is room to expand your fields. There is not one thing to hinder you."

I hunted for words to turn their thinking into another direction.

"Tribemates, I know that I am greatly indebted to you. I revere the memory of Father. When I learned the way he died, great sadness overwhelmed me. But first it is necessary that you understand the kinds of trouble which caught me. The proverb says, 'If you keep feeding the rat your mush long enough, he'll come looking for what's left on your lips.'

"I fed evil until it came back and destroyed me. It caused me to become such a useless thing that the only work which pleased me was to torment and abuse people. I was as one lost forever. No one on earth had power to help me. Only the Great Elder Spirit of our ancestors had mercy on me. I swore to Him that if He would help me, I would serve Him all of my days. He revealed Himself to me. He erased my old evil affairs. He turned my heart around. He delivered me from prison. Because of the hard work He has done for me, I am among you now.

"I came home because I wanted to see you, truly. But I did not come home to marry wives, and to inherit the wealth of my father, and to enter into the chieftainship of our clan. I came home for one little matter. It is my desire that you help me find one wife. Then I expect to return to Luebo to begin the work of teaching people the words of the God of our forefathers."

My words sank in slowly, like water on dried clay.

"Then you are turning your back onto your kingdom?"

"I have a debt to my tribe and to my clan, true. I am the firstborn also. But I have a surpassing debt to the Great Elder Spirit. It is a debt that will bind me forever. He wants me to be His herald. He has called me into the work of His kingdom. That is the inheritance I long for.

"I am no longer seeking a kingdom among people on earth. All my father's other children are not bad. Let the best one of them take Father's place among you. It no longer fits me."

119

The elders muttered among themselves.

"Once he craved honor and wealth; now he is despising them both."

"Let's not judge him hastily; even if your child burns the house down, you won't throw him into the river."

"Let him think about it for awhile; then we'll speak to him again."

X   X   X   X

If my uncles wanted to help me find a wife, they did not show it by their acts. They thought that there was lots of time. So I walked around looking for one myself. But women saw the scar rings on my ankles and elbows, and shook their heads. "Our eyes have verified the truth," they would say. "Why dispute about a pig having a snout?"

For two whole months I walked through the villages of my people hunting. No woman would have me. My heart was splitting. Would I never have my own wife and children and a home? The thought, like green mangoes, made my insides ache. Only God could arrange such a matter. And I vowed in my heart to pay any price for His help.

"Father," I prayed one day, "You know one man can never start a family tree. In that bag of happinesses you said was waiting for me at home, isn't there a wife? Is this the way I'm to be forever? When I find a woman who accepts me, marred and scarred as I am; when I find a woman who doesn't care that the ghost of a slain man is on my body; I'll know that woman is a gift from You. To thank You, for as long as I live, she won't have to work for me; I'll work for her. I'll praise your name forever."

One day a cousin said to me, "There is a young widow in our village; she has born no children. Her father is dead. She sits alone with her mother. She is a good worker; she knows how to make her hoe eat bushes."

"Let's go see her," I said.

We found her seated at her house. My friend started talking.

"Nyembe, my cousin here would like to marry you."

120

Her eyes took a picture of me.

"Where has he been all this time, as old as he is, and still single?"

He mumbled as if his mouth were filled with a chicken bone. He didn't want to ruin everything. Finally he said, "He was in prison."

"Tell me the truth now; for what reason was he in prison?"

He hunted for a soft word, and failed.

"For killing a person."

She said, "Go talk with my elder brother."

My heart leaped. It would be his business to arrange things. I prayed, "Oh my God, the moment you allow me to see a friendship meal of mush and chicken on the table in that man's house, I'll know the contract is sealed."

When we arrived and told the brother what we wanted, he said, "Come back in the morning."

I went to my room in Uncle Kazadi's house and prayed with all my strength. "Father," I said, "tomorrow give me a wife. Why would You let me suffer like this forever, me belonging to You?"

The next day, December 9, 1953, we ate the meal and agreed on bride price. I went back to my room, got onto my knees, and said, "My Father, I pour out my thanks to You. I'll glorify You perpetually."

I learned that a friend had gone to visit my wife-to-be during the night.

"That man has become a person of God," he told her. "He doesn't have all those old affairs with him any longer. There's no ghost of a dead person going to accuse him anymore."

But if Nyembe was willing to have me, her mother was not. Someone carried word to her. She raised her voice and began the yodeling call of one wailing the dead.

"Nyembe, my only girl-child, they've delivered you into the hands of a people-stealer for the white man."

"Mother, have you ever seen that kind of business with your eyes? When it is written for me to die, I'll die, whether I'm in your hands, or in the hands of my husband."

"But what about the ghost that is on him?"

121

"If that ghost ever has power to kill me, it will be because the God of our fathers has already decided that it is time for me to die."

There was no comfort in these words for her mother.

"My child, the day you die in the hands of that man, I'll go to the one who told him about you; I'll burn his house down, and we'll die together."

In the days that followed, we completed the marriage contract, according to tribal custom.

I told Nyembe, "I feared there was no woman on earth who would accept me. I promised God that if He brought me a wife, she would not need to serve me as the custom is; instead, I would serve her. Don't be upset that I keep such a vow. Just sit quietly and keep your peace. Because you felt in your heart to accept me as I am, God be praised."

My clan mates did not come to talk with me again. They watched me bring firewood from the forest, my wife sitting idle at the hut. They watched us come from the field, me carrying a basket of cassava on my head, Nyembe empty-handed. They saw me bring corn from the field, husk it, shell it, and take it to the mill for grinding.

By the time we left for Luebo, they just sat and watched me pass back and forth among them. To me they were silent; but to one another they were shaking their lips. Friends my own age informed me.

"We had thought that Maweja was a man of loyal heart; a man to be counted on. We wanted to make him a man of renown. Look at him now. He's become a fool. He's stupid. He's worthless. He is renouncing chieftainship. Didn't he see with his own eyes how his father was rich because of the work of his wives? Maweja; a child of the clan of Kaseki of Tshiyamba; big enough to rout our enemies. 'The all-powerful one.'

"He is renouncing the wealth of his father! He doesn't want wives to work for him. Nyembe has a strong body; he doesn't even want her to work for him. Since people began being born on earth, has anyone ever heard of a man working for his wife? Haven't we seen him? He is harvesting the crops for her! What kind of woman is she with power to make that big man work for her? An incredible affair!

"When he was gone away from us, he despised the laws of the ancestors, and look at all the troubles that caught him. What misfortune will catch him now, his turning their laws around backwards like this? He's a rebel. One living among us who so defies tradition will only bring ills and misfortune to us all. Only a few days ago he came to us a person greatly honored; now in leaving, he brings us shame."

I kept my peace. I knew what I had promised Christ. I kept on doing the work that was mine to do. God said I was worth something. He was counting on me. There was nothing as important to me as that.

It seemed I was so full of His grace that offenses of my family did not bother me. I kept my heart stuck to the words of the Bible which say, "Don't take your vows lightly; perform them" (Matthew 5:33); and "When you make a vow to God, don't fail to keep it; God isn't happy with fools" (Ecclesiastics 5:4).

My Christian Walk Alienates Many **20**

Thus I broke my ties with the people of Tshiyamba. I crossed the river that divided me from their ways, and they took the dugout boat home with them.

This is no light affair. Our tribal people are accustomed to depending upon one another for everything they need. When one cuts himself off from them, who remains for him to depend on? My people shook their heads and said, "There are too many hazards on such a path; he is bound to stumble."

But in my seeing it, the path ahead of me was bright and plain. God was giving me the affirmation in my heart that what I had done pleased Him. Whenever a person must make a choice, and he pledges in his heart to choose and follow what is right, he will find courage to surmount all obstacles, and afterward, he will be recompensed with joy.

I had already lived away from home for many years; it was not an overwhelming problem for me. But it was not thus with Nyembe. She had always lived in the village. Any place beyond our tribal land was foreign to her. For the things she needed, she had always trusted friends and relatives; people close to her, whom she knew could be relied upon. But now, for some reason surpassing comprehension, she chose to be abandoned by those she had always trusted, and to tie herself to a strange man whose body was scarred with his evil, and whose hands were red with a dead person's blood, to go anywhere in the world he led her. Truly, she had a heart of great courage and trust.

This meant that we had to start a new way of living. We could no longer rely upon our clan mates. The only one left to rely upon was our Father in heaven.

I was indebted to Nyembe. The obligation now caught me to prove to her that I loved her and meant her no harm, that our Father could be relied upon to bring us the things we needed, and that those who are members of His tribe have a new set of laws they must follow. During the first years of our marriage, we learned together the blessings and responsibilities of this new life.

Nyembe, two small children of one of her relatives, and I began the return journey to Luebo. Only a few days remained for class to begin. We arrived at the train station. I went to the ticket window.

"Give me four tickets—two for grown-ups; two for children."

"Do you have a path letter?"

"What kind of path letter?"

"No one can get onto the train for such a journey without a letter of authorization from the government man. Next person."

The words shattered my hopes like a hammer striking a clay pot. In what way could I possibly get such a letter? Government authorities see people only at certain hours. One stands in line a long time to see them. Even if I waited to see one, he would probably say, "Your name is not on the census-list of people living here. Who are you?" That would lead to other matters which would mix up things worse. But I had to board the train. What would happen if I did not arrive at Luebo in time for the beginning of class?

"They're asking for a path letter," I told Nyembe and the children. "I have no way of getting it. In the middle of battle, all the warriors rely upon their champion. We're not going to eat anything tonight. We'll have to rely upon God alone to arrange this path letter business."

We walked to a nearby village to find a place to sleep. That night I went outside to be alone. "Father, you see the trouble we're having," I prayed. "I'm Your bond slave. I'm not giving allegiance to anyone other than You. Now I need to begin this journey so that I can learn how to do the work You've called me to do. If long time ago in Babylon You closed the mouths of the lions for Your servant Daniel, then tomorrow morning close the mouths of those clerks in the ticket office so they don't trouble me any further about a path letter. When they see my face, make them give us tickets."

That night we slept with hunger.

Early next morning we returned to the station. I showed my face at the ticket window, and asked to buy tickets.

"Do you have a path letter?"

"I am a stranger from Luebo; I've only come to get my wife and these children."

He began writing out our tickets. "Jehovah be praised forever!" my insides shouted. I wanted to split for joy. Nyembe and the children were watching. When I showed them the tickets, they said, "Truly truly, the God you worship does amazing things."

We arrived at Luebo. During our first days there, Nyembe and I spoke our vows of marriage to each other before God in the big temple on the mission station. Those in charge of the Bible School showed us to one of the small houses for students, which was to be our home. I began my studies.

People of all tribes of earth understand the happiness of a man and woman who have just entered marriage. But I did not want my giving myself to happiness with my wife to compete with my commitment to God. In the past, the pleasures of my body had been a big trap to me; I would not allow them to overpower me and cause me to stumble again. I explained to Nyembe.

"I know what my responsibility is to you as my wife; I don't want you to think that I am neglecting it. At the same time, there is nothing I want more than for God to speak to me a message. He must find the way to make me into the kind of worker He hopes for me to be. When Samuel slept in the

126

temple at Shilo, God sent him a message. I want to be like Samuel. At nighttime when others go to bed, I want to go stay in the temple. Jesus said, 'If anybody wants to be my disciple, let him deny himself and follow me.' Let's test His words and see what He'll do for us."

"Let it be as you wish," she said. "Even if you're not at home. I'll know what you are doing."

Thus I began a custom which I followed almost every night during the two and one-half years I went to school. At the time of night when people stop walking around and go to their homes, I went to the temple of God.

While the hours passed, I knelt at a bench, or sat and bowed my head in worship. I told God, "I don't have a thing to bring in my hands to offer You. I beg You to accept me, just the way I am here; only give me the joy of working for You. You found me when my imprisonment was severe. My own sins had put me there. Now I offer myself to You; take me and put me into the same kind of imprisonment for You."

I would stay there until my heart felt at peace. Sometimes I slept there. If people want an explanation for the power with which I have preached and taught the Word of God up to this moment, it is because of those nights when I waited before God in His temple.

When we arrived at Luebo, I continued the custom of working for my wife. The two children would help me. I brought her firewood from the forest. I brought her greens from the garden. I took cassava and corn to the mill to grind. She did the cooking.

People don't like a way of doing things which upsets their customs. They began to gossip about me, saying the same things elders in my home village had said.

Because of the work I did for my wife, I was often with women. Perhaps this custom stirred up trouble in their own homes; perhaps they were jealous of Nyembe's good fortune; perhaps they were accusing their husbands of heartlessness because they had to work while she rested, and their husbands would not change. They began to offend me to my face. They called me every kind of name their minds could create which would kindle my wrath and weaken my heart. Then they began offending Nyembe.

"When you work for me while I sit idle, you make me feel ashamed," she said once. "They say I'm lazy; I am one in value with a dead post sitting in the yard all the time."

"We no longer have a debt to the traditions of an earthly tribe. We now are giving all of our allegiance to another Chief. We belong to His tribe. It is no longer our duty to do what makes us happy, or to do what makes other people happy. It is our duty to do what makes our Chief happy. When we know what pleases Him, we do it with courage, paying no attention to how we feel or to what persons say. Jesus said that if we are offended for His name, we are to rejoice; He'll recompense us greatly. If we have really stuck ourselves to Christ, then what people say doesn't hurt us; it hurts Christ. The elders used to say, 'Don't feel badly if they laugh at you; that's proof you are alive. Feel badly if they are mourning.'

"People will talk. Attach no value to what they say. Sit quietly and be at peace. You cook. You will bear and raise children. I'm going to keep on working for you because when I do thus, I'm finishing my vow; I know I'm pleasing God. I plan to keep right on doing it until I die."

The tramping of many feet smooths the path. So, after the passing of days, people began to show us compassion. When the mill owner looked at the long line of persons waiting to grind their grain or cassava, and saw only one person wearing pants among all those women, he would call me and grind my grain so I could leave right away. When no ill came that men could blame me for, they began saying, "Truly, he must be doing it because he is a child of God." After a whole year passed, women began saying, "Let's stop offending him; it doesn't do any good; that must just be the way he is."

When we were married about a year, Nyembe gave birth to a girl; but during those months she had been anemic. Now at childbirth, she came to the edge of death. I pleaded with my Father, "The way I once abused my powers of bringing birth, I marvel to see this little child. You have been merciful. Now, if You see it is good to leave me alone with it and to take its mother, I won't accuse You of doing wrong. But we're a long way from home. My people say, 'Your in-laws measure your worth by the promises you keep.' If word reaches Nyembe's mother that she has died, her mother will say, 'It's just as I said; she didn't die as all people die; that man delivered her over to the white people-eaters.' I will become a liar in their eyes, and Your name will be dishonored. And by what means will I ever find another woman who will live with me? If You are willing, look upon us in our trouble and have mercy. Raise my wife to life, so that she can go home and sit face-to-face with her mother again, and my promises about You will be affirmed."

A few hours passed. Nyembe woke up and said, "My sickness has subsided." During the weeks that followed, missionaries would give me fresh meat to prepare for her. Her strength returned.

When my days of studying were about finished, our daughter became ill. The doctor said she had intestinal worms. One morning they gave her medicine. She became terribly ill. At noon she died. She was eighteen months old. Nyembe and I broke into mourning.

Then in my heart I saw the eyes of Jesus looking at me with much love. I remembered my promise while in prison: "If You take me out of these chains, whatever appears before me in the days ahead that You want to claim, it is Yours." I continued with sadness; but no longer did I feel the need to weep.

The next day was Sunday. I did not sit in a loin cloth with ashes on my head as mourners ordinarily do. I put on my good clothes. We buried the child. Then, like other people, I went to the temple of God to worship.

People were perplexed. "His child died yesterday; and today he goes to church?" they asked each other.

"That child's death was not a matter of today," I replied. "The day of her death was already fixed before she was ever born."

In the years since then, Nyembe has borne me nine children, one after another. All are living.

Thus during our time at Luebo, Nyembe and I learned

together the laws and traditions of our Lord; we learned the happinesses and obligations of being members of His tribe. Nyembe entrusted herself to me in all that happened. My heart was comforted. God had given me a loyal helpmate for His work. When she was baptized, we named her "Ruth"; she was willing to forsake her mother and leave her home village to go with a stranger to a land she had never seen.

My studies ended in June 1956. Believers in the river-port city of Ilebo asked me to come be their evangelist-teacher. With great joy, I began the work of God; and with perseverance, I fought the war of the Christian.

God Makes Me To Triumph **21**

I cannot be a person of Jesus and give my obedience to the devil. So long as I live in the devil's kingdom and refuse to obey his rules, he will persecute me. The Christian who has no war within himself has made a truce with the devil. The Christian who is loyal to Jesus will be fighting against the authority of the devil to the day of his death.

A person who has been ruled by demons of sin cannot renounce their authority in a single day. Each one of us is different. The devil knows the places where a person is weak. To bring that person into bondage, the devil will send into war those demons which will be able to overthrow that person at his weak places. I cannot reveal to you your weak places; but among mine were anger, pride, and lust for women. It is my desire to share with you my wisdom on how to subdue the demons which the devil sends to war against us.

I have not won all my battles. There would be little help in my relating to you the many times I have failed. But I have now fought this war in my body for many years. I have learned to tie myself to certain rules which give me power to control these troublesome demons. I am no longer under their authority. I have learned to be master of myself, and so am truly a person of freedom. Did not Jesus promise us in John 8:32 that His truth would set us free?

Because we are in these human bodies and have been placed

upon this earth, we see and feel everything around us. We say that these things are real. But we must understand that now we are not talking about matters of this earth. We are talking about matters of the Spirit.

It is also necessary to understand that matters of the Spirit are just as real as those we can look at. Jesus compared them with the wind; we cannot see it, but there is no person who doubts that it is real (John 3:7-8). If we work together with the rules of the wind, it will help us gain the things we need. When the village needs meat, hunters set fire to the grass in the direction from which the wind is coming; the wind sends the fire across the prairie, and drives from it all the animals. As is true with the wind, so it is true with matters of God's Spirit.

We can lay hold on these truths and make them work for us only because we see them with our spiritual eyes. Paul prays that our eyes to perceive spiritual things be unblinded, that we comprehend matters of the Spirit (Ephesians 1:18). Unless the eyes of your heart are open to recognize that these things are real and are to be trusted in, the meaning of the words which follow will be concealed in fog.

If we want to subdue the demons which keep troubling us, we must submit ourselves to three truths of the Spirit.

First, when I gave myself to Jesus, the old Maweja was slain. Like Jesus, he was nailed onto the cross and died there. I have no debt to the old Maweja. His affairs came to an end. A new person has replaced the old one inside this body. The life that I have now, I have because of the faith I keep fixed into Jesus, who loved me, who gave Himself for me, and who is now living inside of me.[54]

Second, because I have given myself to Jesus and He has made me His person, it is no longer mine to do what I wish, or what my friend wishes, or what the devil wishes; it is mine to do only what God wants, whether it pleases me to do it or not.

Every person has the power to surrender himself to a master of his choice; but from the moment he pledges allegiance to his master, he must truly surrender himself to that master by obeying him in all things. If he is still heeding the voice of another authority, the one he has chosen is not truly his master.

Jesus said that a person cannot serve two masters.[55] He said that if I keep trying to hold onto my own life, I will lose it; but if I surrender it for His sake, I will find it.[56] The person who remains at enmity toward the desires of his body will keep it unto eternal life.[57] The earth and all its lusts will perish; but the person who does God's will shall live forever.[58] For this reason, I do not do whatever my body wants. I keep bruising and beating my body so that it knows who its master is. I keep disciplining myself to always do what pleases my Master.[59]

Look at the example Jesus left us. When He was in Gethsemane it was shown Him what great suffering lay ahead. He said, "Father, please take this cup away from me; but let Your will be done."[60] In other words, Jesus did not do what His body wanted; He did what His Father wanted.

That is why I say we cannot do what we want. We are indebted to do what God wants. What I choose to do cannot be for my own happiness. It must be what will glorify Christ in my body. When God sees that we are giving Him this kind of obedience, then He can accord to us power we need to win in our battle with sin.

If a chief knows that his subjects are truly loyal; if he knows that they try to do whatever he asks of them, whether it pleases them or not, he can lead them into battle with great courage. But the enemy will triumph at that point where a warrior has weak loyalty, where he is giving attention to another master. And so, at that place where my obedience is weak, at that same place my power is escaping, and there the enemy will defeat me.

Third, because I have given the whole of myself to Jesus, He has made me His property. He has put me inside of Himself, so that whatever matter hits me really falls upon Him. Because the old Maweja died, and a new person with Jesus was raised to life, I try to not let my mind get snared in the temptations and testings of earthly affairs. I discipline it to fix itself upon matters of the heavenly kingdom.[61]

Drunkenness, pride, immorality, gluttony, anger, the worship of false gods, and such matters are the works of our flesh-bodies. The Bible says that if we train our minds to follow matters of the Spirit, the power of such things will be destroyed.[62] I do not destroy their power; I do not have strength to destroy it. Christ who is living inside my body does it with His power.

My already having accepted that these things are true, when temptation comes, what do I do?

Our faith in these truths is an adequate shield to stand up against our enemy.[63] When demons pick up different kinds of stones of evil and throw them at me, if my faith weakens, then these things will wound me, and leave me with their scars. If I really have faith that these things are true, then I will not be hurt by them. My ears have been taken by the Spirit. My eyes have been taken by the Spirit. My hands and feet have been taken by the Spirit. The stones are not striking me; they are striking Jesus.

When the devil comes and wants to invade a part of my life, I tell him, "I've already delivered my life over into the hands of Jesus. I have no way to take it away from Him and put it back into the path that you desire; you'll have to go talk with Him." Then I begin bruising my body that it quit lusting after that thing; I stick myself to the words of Jesus by praying and surrendering myself to Him. So, by truly keeping myself under the lordship of Jesus, and by believing with persistence that these rules of the Spirit are true, I come to subdue the demons of sin which war against me.

When the living Christ called me to begin doing His work, whenever I saw a person playing with the name of Jesus or ruining His cause, such anger would catch me that I wanted to lay hands on him. I kept continually praying to God, "You know this thorn is aggravating me. Now You've given me the work of leadership. If I keep on acting like this, people who are weak in Jesus will say, 'Our leader still has fangs; he hasn't yet been subdued.' "

There is one path which must be followed if a person wishes to subdue any such thing. He must keep renouncing it; he must keep giving himself anew to Jesus by establishing and affirming his place inside of Jesus; and he must keep feeding himself on the kind of food that comes from heaven.[64]

A bird does not build its nest in a day. It perseveres day after day until the work is done. So I do not worry about the many days it might take to finish this work; Jesus said the troubles of today are sufficient to work with.[65] So by prayer and surrender and obedience, I fight the war that confronts me today; and when I triumph in battle today, I know that I have progressed a little toward that time when the work will be finished.

A person who perseveres in such a course can always affirm in his heart the peace Christ has promised him, though he is in war. He can keep on growing until he is filled with the fullness of all that he needs, and is master of himself.

Let me give you some examples of how these rules of the Spirit have worked in my life.

During my first years of working as pastor, one evening I had a meeting with the elders of my church. When one of them arrived, I saw that he was drunk. Anger rose within me quickly. Then he began insulting me.

"You can't play around with us. We are mature people. You are still a child."

I got up, seized a church bench, and lifted it into the air. "Do you see this?" I asked him. "If I were still caught in affairs of the world, I would bust you into pieces like a church bench for insulting me like that. But I want you to understand that, when I accepted Jesus, I left behind all such affairs. But they are still inside of me here, fighting to overpower me."

I seized his arm and took him to the door. He left by himself. At that time I still wanted to answer insults with anger.

Some years passed. One morning a young man whom I recognized arrived at my house. He was drunk and under drugs.

"The Spirit of God is upon me; the Spirit of God has seized me," he kept saying. Then he began insulting me.

"That kind of spirit . . . did you get it from me?" I asked.

"Yes," he replied. "This is the Spirit I got from you." He kept compounding his offenses to make me angry.

I stayed inside of Jesus and kept repeating to myself the words of Jehovah: "Who is blind like my servant? Who is deaf like the messenger I have sent?" [66]

This continued to noon. When I went into my house to eat,

he began crying out, "You're not to eat. The Spirit is telling me. Don't touch your food. Give me the key to your car. I want to use it."

I went outside to try and quiet him. When I got close, he slapped me hard on the side of my face, piyaaaaaaaaaa. Those eating inside the house got up and came running. My children began crying.

"Don't harm him," I said. "He has no affair. It is not he that struck me. It is the devil who is inside of him."

We put the man into my car. I drove him to the doctor.

"Bring him back at two o'clock," the doctor said.

I took him to the police station.

"Lock this person up until two o'clock; if I let him loose the way he is, he may kill somebody," I said.

"We can't put him with other prisoners; we've got nothing to bind him with," they replied.

I drove the man to his home. His wife and children and relatives where there. "Where has he been?" they asked. "We've been hunting him all day. What's the matter with him?" I put him into their hands and told them they were responsible to keep him from harming anyone. I left.

At two o'clock I got him and took him to the clinic. The doctor began giving him injections and feeding him pills. After a time he got his good senses back and began to cry.

"Why did I strike our pastor? I was a fool. People deceived me. They said, 'Here's $60.00. We want to put pastor to the test. Go beat up on him. When he strikes you back, fall to the ground and play dead. They we'll come to rescue you. We'll beat up on pastor and plunder his house. We'll see if he can restrain himself or not.' I took dope and drank to get courage to do it."

I kept my peace. This example attracted many people. "What kind of person, slapped like that, can remain silent?" they asked. God used this incident to bring many people to give themselves to Jesus.

You will remember the time I spent a day with a young girl in a compartment on the train. I almost stumbled into sin. She was innocent. But there are women in my country with evil hearts who lay traps to seduce men.

Because of my licentious living when I was young, there has been no battle more fierce than this one. Whenever such a woman accosts me, I see her as an envoy of Satan sent personally to test me. I cannot say that I will never again fail with a woman for as long as I live. But so long as I follow the rules of the Spirit, I will not.

The battle is no longer as fierce as it once was. When such a woman comes to me now, it is my custom to reply, "You want me to go to bed with you? Another day you'll come asking me to pray for you. How will I pray for you if I've gone to bed with you? What right would I have to pray for you? How could I pray for God to help you when I need His help as badly as you, and I myself haven't yet received it?" After asking them such questions, they go on their way.

Before I went to prison, people praised me, and pride drove me to act like a crazy man. Even so today, the praise of people is a snare. Often when I speak to pastors I oversee, I tell them, "If you are competing for honor; if you want to come out ahead of everyone else in being accorded praise, listen to me. Long ago the disciples had the same desire. Jesus answered them, 'If you don't turn your hearts around and become like little children, you won't even enter into the kingdom of heaven. The one who humbles himself most as a little child, that person will surpass the greatness of all others in the kingdom of heaven'" (Matthew 18:1-4).

People who live like this are not manifesting weakness. They are manifesting maturity. I saw this happen before my eyes when Christ turned my heart around in prison. I longed to prove to the prisoners that I loved them. Though my understanding was small at that time, I began serving them. After a time, my humbling myself in this manner made me a strong person among them; it drained from us the poison of wanting perpetually to do one another evil, and caused us to love one another. When humbling ourselves has power to do such amazing things, is it surprising that those with humility will be the greatest in the kingdom of God?

We who are in the Church, we need to imagine that we are in

a class. When the teacher puts a test on the board, no student ever says to another, "Try hard to get a higher mark than I." Never. Each pupil strives to put himself ahead of all the others. I tell my pastors, I tell my elders, I tell my wife, that each of us must do his own striving to have the kind of humility that will make him come out greater than all the others. Each person will win his place, in proportion to his humility.

By doing this, people show that they are strong and mature. They will not be jealous of one another. They will not be arguing with one another. Each will be growing surpassingly in his wanting to win; and all will grow together.

The eyes of the Lord wander to and fro over the whole earth, so that He can show His might toward those whose hearts are completely His.[67] When He sees our desire to follow the rules of the Spirit, He will pour out His grace upon us. He has poured out His grace upon my family. Our children have learned to love Him.

When they began growing up, I explained to them why I am as a servant to their mother. My scars showed them the truth of my words. They were taught how to work. Now, many times I am on journey to oversee the work of other pastors or to do the work of evangelism. At such times, I arrange with my older children to carry the burden of work at home. One of my sons is studying in the university. When Nyembe is not busy with the smaller children, she organizes and strengthens the work of God among different groups of women here and there.

God has also poured out His grace upon my teaching of His Word. He has fulfilled my longing in prison to teach great numbers of people. I began work in the river-port city of Ilebo in June of 1956. The church grew. I was ordained as pastor. When the troubles of political independence caught us, I could not stay there.

In May of 1961 I touched my feet down at the city of Mwena Ditu in my own tribal country. When I was called to begin work in the church there, it had about seven hundred members. Along the roads leaving the city were villages with thousands of people. Many were refugees; they like me and my family, had fled fighting in other places and had returned to their tribal home country. No places of worship had yet been established among them.

In 1963 we established a church at Makota; a large number worship there. In 1968 we gave birth to a church at Tshibangu Mpata; three to four hundred people are worshipping there. Then we began Kadela, which now has two hundred members. In 1973 we bore Tshiamala where about one hundred worship. Now we are about to establish a church at Musawula with about two hundred beginning members.

All of these churches have chosen their own elders and deacons; most have their own pastors. Whenever we see a large number of people beginning to come to a church from a long distance, we say, "You people are strong and mature in your faith. Why don't we help you establish a place of worship in your home village?" Members of my own church in Mewna Ditu now number one thousand eighteen hundred.

So our joy grows, in proportion to the number of children we bear; and the Great Elder Spirit of my ancestors continues to use me in His work.

In the beginning I was a child of Tshiyamba, a son of slavery. I became caught in the slavery of sin. Then I discovered the One whose truth was hidden in my forefathers' customs. He liberated me. Now, in the end, it is my surpassing joy to live in His slavery and to see others set free.

Epilogue

The last night Levi Keidel spent with Pastor Maweja was on August 27, 1974. They slept in a room of the Protestant Centre in Kananga, Zaire. It was a restless night. Maweja got in and out of bed repeatedly. Finally he spent a long time closeted in the lighted bathroom. Keidel began to wonder if Maweja was worried that he might have shared too many intimate experiences. At 5 a.m. Keidel turned on the light, thanked Maweja for his collaboration, and assured him that he would not reveal information of a nature which could damage his ministry. Following is Maweja's reply.

No, Levi; I'm not worried about the things I've related to you. I want to speak of matters which give me great heaviness in my heart. I have a burden which I want to share with the people of America.

The distress I have is about the Church; the burden I carry day after day is for my fellow-Zairians who are Christians. How can we find those who will renounce bondage to their sins and serve Jesus with all their strength? How can we bring them to the place where they will submit themselves to God in the manner He expects? After we have worked on this earth the years of our lives, what kind of people will we have in our hands to present to Christ?

There are a few who give me great joy: Pastor Nkashala in the capital city; Pastor Kabangu at Katanda. Do you remember Likasi, the city where I was first in prison for six months? Pastor Mbayi, a child I have born in Christ, is working there now. Three elders also are struggling hard to follow my footsteps. When any of them stands before a crowd to teach, people say, "He's a child of Maweja; we'll feed well today."

I can't judge what is going on inside a person. But among our pastors, I don't see many who have truly submitted themselves to the rules of the Spirit and are echoing the life of Jesus. Greed, rivalry, jealousy and gossip are still found among them.

When an important government authority from Kinshasa comes to visit our city, officials send word: "We want Maweja to come to represent the church." Some pastors say to each other, "That meek Maweja; does he have the kind of demeanor which will properly represent us to leaders of our government?"

Children imitate their parents. So Christians imitate their leaders. The Bible says, "You have taken off your old manner of living which was being rotted by lust; you have put on the new man which imitates God and is being created in righteousness and purity" (Ephesians 4:22-24). I used to talk, see and think like the devil. But now that I am baptized and have put on Christ, who am I acting like? If we still fornicate, lust, fight and compete, where is the sign that we have taken off our old manner of living? Where is the sign that we are strangers in the kingdom of an enemy?

People are content to remain in bondage to sin because they don't have spiritual eyes. Man lost the eyes of his spiritual senses when our ancestors obeyed the words of Satan in Paradise. Man hasn't been able to see since.

Jesus called the Pharisees "blind leaders." They said, "We're blind? Look at all the pretty buildings here in Jerusalem. This youth is telling us we're blind? He's insulting us." Jesus said, "I came that those who see be blind, and that the blind may see" (John 9:39). Jesus came onto earth for this purpose: to return to us the eyes we lost in Eden.

After Paul met Jesus on the Damascus road, Ananias gave him new eyes; then he could see the truth of his past, present and future. Then Jesus told him, "I'm sending you to the Gentile tribes to open their eyes, so that they may turn from darkness to light, and from the kingdom of Satan to the kingdom of God (Acts 26:16-18).

To bring people to the place where they will open their hearts is hard. Jesus said, "He who hears my commandments and keeps them, my Father will love him; we will come into him and make our home inside of him" (John 14:23). They refuse. Because if they obey, their new eyes will give them knowledge that will demand that their whole manner of living be changed into the love path. We can't pull them there with the strength of our arms and bodies; we can't bribe them to come there by putting money into their hands. It is something they must say "Yes" to; then God puts it inside of them.

My heart was weighted with this burden when I went to America. There I saw rows and rows of people who had gone to church all of their lives until their hair was white and their bodies were feeble. I heard them pray. I saw the hospitals and schools and homes for old people that their money has built.

When I got back home, I was thinking much about these things. Some important people among us have money. Do we ever hear that one of them has built a hospital or church or school building? No. They build nightclubs and bars . . . places which bring rottenness into society.

Do we have those who persevere in going to church until their heads are white? A few. Most persevere in drinking, adultery, pride and factionalism. What glory is in being experts in such things?

Now some among us have even arrived at not wanting to acknowledge God. What of value is left in a tribe when it no longer has God?

When I remembered what Christians in America are doing, and saw how we in Zaire are, I cried out to God, "When will we come to be like that?" He showed me that you have known Him for centuries; there are roots so long and so deep that His business has gotten into your blood and skin and bones. It took

Him many years to deliver me from bondage. With the passing of more years, He will deliver others.

So we strengthen our hearts in the war we wage. We strengthen our hearts in the work we do. But inside myself, I am always mourning. Sometimes I don't sleep well at night. I'm pleading with God that He will give us a few thousand believers in Zaire who have received spiritual eyes, who have subdued their demons of sin, and who rejoice to be slaves of Jesus with us.

I have shared with you my burden. I leave you with a debt: Pray for us in Zaire.

Footnotes

[1] Sources of information for chapters two and three beyond personal interviews are Histoires Des Buluba, F. Lazare-M. Mpoyi, Institute St. Jean B., Mbuji Mayi, Zaire; and Sons of Muntu, thesis of David A. McLean, Chairman, Dept. of Anthropology, St. Andrews Presbyterian College, Laurenburg, N.C.

[2] Chapters four through six depict the nature of tribal life during Maweja's childhood. Specific incidents have been structured to show the application of tribal law and tradition to daily living.

[3] Compare Matthew 27:45-51. Interestingly, according to ancient records, earthquake and inexplicable darkness occurred simultaneously among the Mayan and Inca peoples of Mexico, and in Greece, Rome and Egypt. Historians Phlegon and Tertullian described it as a "universal darkness" engulfing Europe and Asia.

[4] Tshiyamu Meupela Nzala Lufu Kaluena Kuepela.

[5] Simon Kimbangu was arrested by Belgian colonial authorities in 1921 and was imprisoned to his death in 1951. He is the founder of the most popular indigenous religious movement in Zaire, the Church of Jesus Christ on Earth through the Prophet Simon Kimbangu, whose adherents currently are said to approximate one million.

[6] Proverbs 28:13; [7] I John 1:8; [8] Matthew 11:28; [9] Judges 1:26; [10] I Samuel 9:16; [11] II Chronicles 14:1; [12] Genesis 17:12; [13] Numbers 35:33-34. Leviticus 18:25, Hosea 4:2-3; [14] Genesis 4:10-11; [15] I Kings 21:19-21, 22:37-38, II Kings 9:21-26; [16] Job 20:27; [17] Exodus 12:13; [18] Leviticus 24:19, Exodus 21:24-25; [19] Numbers 5:12ff; [20] Deuteronomy 22:22-29, Exodus 22:16-17; [21] Leviticus 20:9, Joshua 7:24-25; [22] Job 20: 20-29; [23] Genesis 29:18; [24] Genesis 24:10; [25] Hosea 3:1-2; [26] Deuteronomy 25:5; [27] Genesis 38:14; [28] Genesis 21:10; [29] Genesis 1:28; [30] Genesis 24:60; [31] Psalm 127:3-5; [32] Genesis 27:34-35, 48:13-18, Deuteronomy 21:17; [33] Leviticus 15:28-30; [34] Genesis 30:16; [35] Genesis 16:5, I Samuel 1:6, 2:1-5; [36] Genesis 9:20-25, Leviticus 18:6-71; 20:20-22; [37] Leviticus 12:2-6; [38] Genesis 17:5; [39] Genesis 32:28; [40] Genesis chapter 30; [41] Luke 1:31; [42] Exodus 15:1-21; [43] Deuteronomy 32:1-43; [44] Judges chapter 5; [45] I Samuel 2:1-10; [46] Genesis 50:3; [47] Deuteronomy 34:8; [48] Mark 5:38-39; [49] Nehemiah 2:3-5; [50] Leviticus 17:11, Hebrews 9:22; [51] Leviticus 14:48-49; [52] Leviticus 16:7-10; [53] Leviticus 23:10-11, 22, Exodus 22:22-24; [54] Galatians 2:20; [55] Matthew 6:24; [56] Matthew 10:39; [57] John 12:25; [58] I John 2:16-17; [59] I Corinthians 9:26-27; [60] Matthew 26:39; [61] Colossians 3:1-3; [62] Galatians 5:16-21; [63] Ephesians 6:16; [64] I Peter 2:1-3; [65] Matthew 6:34; [66] Isaiah 42:19; [67] II Chronicles 16:9.